The Human Image in Dramatic Literature

Francis Fergusson was born in 1904 in New Mexico, where he spent most of his childhood. After three years at Queens College, Oxford, as a Rhodes Scholar, receiving his undergraduate degree in 1926, he entered the American Laboratory Theatre in New York, under the direction of Richard Boleslavsky. Mr. Fergusson, who has been writing theater criticism since 1930, has been on the faculties of The New School for Social Research, Bennington College, where he organized and directed the college theater, Princeton University, Indiana University, and Rutgers University, where he is currently teaching.

Mr. Fergusson is the author of *The Idea of a Theater* (1949), which appears in the Anchor series, and *Dante's Drama of the Mind: A Modern Reading of the Purgatorio* (1953).

The Human Image in Dramatic Literature

ESSAYS BY

Francis Fergusson

DOUBLEDAY ANCHOR BOOKS

DOUBLEDAY & COMPANY, INC.

GARDEN CITY, NEW YORK

Cover designed by Leonard Baskin
Wood engraving by Daumier
Typography by Edward Gorey

Library of Congress Catalog Card Number 57–12464
Copyright © 1957 Francis Fergusson
Printed in the United States of America

ACKNOWLEDGMENTS

Most of the essays in this book have been published before, as follows:

"Three Allegorists," "Two Comedies," "'Myth' and the Literary Scruple," "*The Golden Bowl* Revisited," and "Kenneth Burke's *Grammar of Motives*" in *The Sewanee Review*.

"*Don Perlimplín:* Lorca's Theater-Poetry" and "*Measure for Measure*" in *The Kenyon Review*.

"T. S. Eliot's *Poetry and Drama*" in *The Partisan Review*.

"Boleslavsky's *The First Six Lessons*" in *Hound and Horn*.

"Two Perspectives on European Literature" in *The Hudson Review*.

"*Macbeth* as The Imitation of an Action" in *English Institute Essays 1951* (New York, Columbia University Press, 1952; Copyright 1952, Columbia University Press).

"Joyce's *Exiles*" as the Introduction to the New Directions edition of that play (1946).

"*Don Perlimplín:* Lorca's Theater-Poetry" and "*The Golden Bowl* Revisited" have both been reprinted in *Perspectives USA*.

I wish to thank the editors for permission to reprint here. Much of the material of "Reflections on the Life of the American Theater" has been taken from a lecture given at Barnard College in a series entitled "New Ideals in American Life," and from articles in *The Partisan Review* and *The Kenyon Review*. It has been rewritten for the purposes of this book.

F.F.

Preface

THE essays in this book were written at various times during the last dozen years or more, often on specific assignment. I have arranged them in three groups according to topic: the modern theater, Shakespeare, and critical attitudes. This arrangement is not intended to suggest a complete, coherent view of the theater in our time: the papers collected here are strictly *essays*, tentative soundings of matters which seem to me significant. But a certain conception of what *is* significant in dramatic literature and the theater, and a certain notion of what a critic should try to do, governs them all.

The title I have adopted for the collection, "The Human Image," is intended to suggest this focus. The writer's function, Mr. Allen Tate says in his essay *The Man of Letters in the Modern World,* is "to render the image of man as he is in his time." This formula strikes me as essentially right, all the more so because it echoes Hamlet, who bids the players reflect human nature and the pressure of their times; Dante, who explains that the meaning of the *Divine Comedy,* underlying the fictive journey beyond the grave, is Man in his earthly destiny; and Aristotle, who regards all the arts as imitations in their various media of human life and/or action. I do not apologize for evoking these august presences, even though they make our contemporary cult of Humane Letters look a little weak and lost. For they remind us that the arts of words, whether we recognize it or not, and however deep or shallow they may be, do in fact play a central role in the complicated workings of our culture. I wish to emphasize the centrality of literature, written or spoken: its significance, not only for those who devote their lives to it, but for all who seek to be aware of the human in his changing world.

It is not so easy to say where Literature, in this classic sense, is to be found in our society. Shall we say that Madison Avenue and Broadway have it in their keeping, and that the middle-brow hits and best sellers, being certified by the market, reveal man in our time? Or that the radio and TV, advertising, the comics and the pulps, with their far vaster audience, more truly picture the inner life of the contemporary human? Or shall we insist that the "obscure quarterlies" which endeavor to culti-vate the arts of letters consciously, sustaining and ex-pounding the great and isolated writers, are closer to reality, and not, as they are so often supposed to be, the lunatic fringe? My own choice would be the literary quarterlies, and what they stand for. But there is no general agreement about the place of theater or litera-ture with us, and there is no simple, adequate answer to the questions I have raised. The schizophrenic Eden of the middle-brows, where everyone is nice *and* rich; and the venal daydreams of sentimentality or violence which inform the mass media have their meaning too. The instinct to project images of human life is basic, the fake glamour of advertising is (however remotely) anal-ogous to the vision of the austerest poet: it too may be read as an outward and visible sign of the spirit's life.

If so, then the first effort of the critic must be to sort out the chaos of modern writing according to the depth, the freedom and the candor it reveals. The quality of the art depends on the depth of the artist's life, as Joyce remarked; but that is not to adopt a Platonic conception according to which art is to be judged for its direct moral and political effect. Those who adopt a Platonic philosophy in our time demand that the writer be "engaged"; by which they mean that he must take sides in the current political and philosophical disputes. That view seems to me to deny the nature, and the special value, of poetry or fiction or drama: the poet is of course engaged in human life, and as a citizen he may engage in the party strife of his time, but his vision comes from experience, and not from his political or religious beliefs. Moreover, the value of Poetry lies partly in its peculiar pleasure, and this pleasure involves not only "recognition"—our sense that the writer has confirmed our own inchoate insights—but also the pleasure of form, all that Aristotle meant by "harmony." And, in practice, it is difficult to separate these two aspects of the successful work of art: what it says, and what it *is*, as beautiful object—as play or poem—are one. In short, one must be careful, while insisting on the general significance of literature, to recognize that in its source, its aims, and its methods it is independent of its closest relatives, philosophy, history, and the other arts and sciences which take the human as their object.

It is the lyric poets and their exegetes who have done the most to establish the freedom of their art, and to distinguish Poetry as it would be "in itself" from the thousand mixed and groping forms which the poetizing instinct takes in literature as we know it. This modern defense of the very idea of poetry has been maintained by that distinguished line which goes from Poe to Baudelaire, Mallarmé and Valéry, and then, by way of Pound and Eliot, back to us; to Wallace Stevens, Hart Crane, Marianne Moore, John Crowe Ransom, Allen Tate, R. P. Blackmur, and their colleagues and followers. From their labors emerges the indispensable notion of the poet *as poet*. As a man the poet may and often does cultivate his mind through the study of philosophy, science, theology and history. Like other men he may accept some political or religious creed by faith. And all that he learns and believes will have its effect upon his mind and his sensibility. But the immediate source of his *poetry* is more intimate and more uncommitted than what he learns from others; what he knows as poet is in his own experience.

Professor Jacques Maritain's *Creative Intuition in Art and Poetry* sums up this strictly modern achievement, which may be called "poetry's new self-awareness." Maritain's book seems to show, among many other things, that this achievement is complete. Few contemporary poets still pursue the ideal of "pure" poetry, and the greatest masters of the modern lyric already seem to belong in another generation. But the lore of poetry-in-itself which Maritain sets forth with such sureness and delicacy is one thing the modern critic should accept as firmly established; and he must acquire it as well as he can.

Maritain writes out of his long familiarity with poetry since Baudelaire, but also as philosopher and psychologist, and one of the great values of his work is that he relates the new knowledge of poetry to his own basically Aristotelian conception of man in a real world. The poet's vision is ultimately derived from his human efforts to find his way in the puzzling world we all know, i.e., from experience. But experience, in this sense, is not a matter of literal observation and report; it accumulates slowly within us at some deep level at the very edge of awareness. We can hear its voice only when we are free from the immediate pressures of the environment. It is not easy to be aware of experience: concentration is required as well as detachment. Maritain speaks of the poet, when he tries to fix his inspiration or his vision, as listening with the inner ear. He is listening (or looking) for the accepted experience, which, perhaps because it *has* been accepted, comes to him as a harmony, a form or an order. In this vision, what the poet has wished for and what he has gotten are inextricably mixed: he has a vision of some aspect of human nature *and* destiny.

He has no access, as poet, to mystical or supernatural insight. His realm is where we all are, his material a reflection in his own spirit.

The essays in this book are not concerned with lyric poetry, but with drama and fiction, and no one supposes that these arts could aspire to "pure" poetry in the manner of the great poets' poetry. But (as Maritain and others have pointed out) the dramatist or the novelist, when he really has something to say, also taps the sources of poetry, and tries to be true to them in his own more unregenerate medium. "Tell me what an artist is, and I will tell you of what he has *been* conscious," said Henry James; "thereby I shall express to you at once his boundless freedom and his moral reference." James was thinking of the dramatist or the novelist, but his formula agrees with the wisdom of the modern tradition of Lyric poetry. He insists both upon the artist's freedom—his possession of a unique mode of knowledge—and upon the general significance of what he sees and embodies in his work.

The most satisfactory theory of the spiritual content of art, that vision embodied in it which gives it a more than purely esthetic significance, is Aristotelian. According to this theory, what the artist has been aware of is some action, motive, or "movement of spirit" (as Dante calls it), which has met its fate; and the whole sense of this experience has been accepted. It is this accepted (and therefore ordered) vision which the artist seeks to imitate in his poem, play or novel. One of the advantages of this theory is that it enables one to recognize analogies between all forms of literature. The instinct to "imitate" life as it is felt in experience, and thus to share the pleasures of recognition and harmony, seems to be at work in poetizing of every degree. One may find it in the second-hand, spiritually starved daydreams of the mass media. At the other extreme one may learn to see the human spirit "moving" toward what it craves even in the purest arts, which do not literally picture man at all. Music, the most abstract of arts, has the least direct reference to actual persons or events, but it is music which most intimately conveys the sense of the psyche's movements. Mallarmé sought in his lyrics an intimate but abstract allusiveness like that of music, and in them also one may find a movement of spirit—even though it be the *"refus indéfini d'être quoi que ce soit"*; a quest for absence suggested by images which are evoked only to be denied. Aristotle's theory is sometimes thought to apply only to drama and fiction, where action is imitated literally and unmistakably in characters and events. But it was he who reminded us that character and plot are only means to the artist's end; it is the play or novel as a whole, not the concrete elements that compose it, which gives the artist's meaning. It is the "life" of the whole play or novel that reflects the poet's vision—which, being derived from the accumulation of many experiences, has a *general* significance analogous to that of philosophy. It is in that sense that I speak of the "human image" to be found in drama and fiction. And it is in this sense that the novelist or dramatist taps the sources of poetry, even though when he writes his play or novel the actual world comes back in countless concrete images—as though to persuade us that we were looking at reality itself instead of a reflection in a human spirit.

The reader, and a fortiori the critic, attempts to share the unique life embodied in the play or novel; but what he actually has before him is a work written in the language which the writer inherited. The writer and the reader of good will try to transcend the limitations of the common medium. The most scrupulous writers seek to "purify the language of the tribe": cleanse it of the worn-out clichés and sleazy approximations of everyday usage, and render it capable of serving their purposes more exactly. The critics' labor of love consists largely in the attempt to read the common language as the particular artist has used it. But inherent in this whole enterprise are the ancient and honorable difficulties of the *art* of writing, which come from the intractability of the common language. The artist encounters them at every turn in his effort to write, and the critic in his effort to "read" what the artist has written.

The language the writer has to work with is, of course, so old, tough and complex that even the greatest masters cannot hope to control it completely. The mere vocabulary of English (or French or Spanish, as the case may be) is implicated in the current life of its society and its changing traditions, and beyond that in the manifold heritage of the whole culture. And the novelist or playwright uses not only words, but common "languages" of many other kinds: traditional symbolic systems; scientific or philosophical vocabularies; theatrical conventions. He may use the artificial limitations of genres for his special purposes; he may try for further accuracy through the subtleties of style and implicit attitude. In our time a writer like Joyce or Mann is aware of the unmanageably vast resources of literature. And the critic, if he begins to see how diverse and yet interconnected the languages of literature are, must recognize at once that there is more to know (if he is to read with full understanding) than he can possibly know.

The cult of Humane Letters has its precarious existence in our time between our vast stores of learning one way, and the dim but actual poetizing of the mass media the other way. The instant we turn off the radio—interrupting, perhaps, an interview with a best-selling author mixed with crooning about some glamorous new cigarette—we realize that the libraries and the museums are lying in wait. Or rather we remember, with despair, that they are quietly growing through the Alexandrian labors of the scientific scholar and the *Museum-Mensch*. It is no wonder that in this confusion we tend to despair of Humane Letters in the ancient sense. Many fine minds see that it is "sounder" to preserve an ironic silence about the perennial life and meaning of literature, and serve it in some way which may be more easily recognized and evaluated.

Thus the professional scholars devote themselves to the task of elucidating the languages of literature. The need for the scholar's work is easy to recognize, and to some extent his results may be checked by his colleagues. Educational and "research" foundations recognize scholarly work, and all who seek to read literature, especially that of other times and places, must recognize it also, as an indispensable means to the ends of Humane Letters. But when the scholars, in their search for a proper rigor, rule out as unscientific the perennial meaning of literature, they kill it. Their science or pseudo-science replaces the ancient art, the masterpieces of the past are treated as dead, like the shell of the departed coral animal, which may be safely measured, labeled, classified and laid away for good.

The professional man of letters who, as writer, editor or publisher, finds or "creates" a large enough audience to guarantee him a living, serves literature in a different but equally recognizable way. In so far as literature is alive it must have an audience, not only for economic support, but as one of the bases of the art itself: *Si le lecteur n'éxistait pas, il faudrait l'inventer.* But in the work of this profession also the means tend to obscure the end: that happens when the sense of the market replaces the sense of literature. This substitution is very easy and natural in our confused and cosmopolitan time. It is hard to trust one's own taste, natural to trust the verdict of success or failure as registered in box-office figures and best-seller lists. We all make this reflex response, but when we do we cut the root of a living literary culture.

The market has its authority, it mechanically registers what "goes"; scholarship has its authority, which is like that of some kinds of science. But neither the market diagnostician nor the scholar cultivates the literary art directly; and the authority of the library and the authority of the market combine to make us doubt the validity, or even the existence, of Humane Letters. The critic who tries to read fiction or drama for humane ends, seeking the image of the perennial human beneath "the masquerades which time resumes," cannot, therefore, accept the methods and the criteria of the recognized authorities without betraying the purpose of his peculiar labors. In his effort to read the languages of literature correctly he needs both the lore of the market and the lore of the library. But it is evident that no man can with a straight face pretend to much authority in either realm. The critic must therefore claim, for his efforts to "read" literature, a strictly amateur status. He must renounce the mirage of encyclopedic completeness or "scientific" soundness, and try to cultivate instead a sense of proportion. Confronted by the trackless maze of the past and present languages of literature—all related to each other, all, unfortunately, relevant—the critic must learn to spend his little energies where they will do the most good, distinguishing what is essential in literature from what is accidental, peripheral, trivial, or merely temporary.

Criticism is thus not a science, but rather an art, an empirical skill. It may aspire only to the kind of validity which skill attains. Because Aristotle had so firm a sense of the end, and also of the spiritual content, of literature, he was able to outline, in principle at least, a method for the "reading" of literature which does not betray the essential nature of that art. Thus he recognizes the actual complexity of the languages of literature and drama when he lists the organic parts of the completed work as plot, character, words, spectacle, music and thought. If the critic endeavors to take account of these elements, in the infinitely varying combinations which are possible, with the emphasis shifting from one to another—and all in relation to the artist's end—he will perforce seek *empirical* skill, and he will have to cultivate, like a performer or athlete, a sense of equilibrium and proportion. Aristotle did not confuse literature with science or philosophy, and it was he who remarked that we must seek, in any art or science, only the kind of exactitude which the nature of that art or science permits.

We know that in the last two thousand years the arts which Aristotle contemplated so soberly have sprouted, died, and come up again in countless forms; and we know that everything in the human situation that looked solid to him now looks doubtful or simply illusory. We are led to think that his problem was simpler than ours, and many hasten to add that he can have nothing useful to say to us in our sophisticated age. I prefer to regard his simplicity as immensely valuable: like other Greeks, he was near the roots. The little space of common sense where he made his observations is surrounded by the unknown, but it is still that little space where we live most of our lives, and in it, or through it, we must still communicate, if we do so at all. The contemporary students of literature who have done the most to restore the notion of Humane Letters, and to elucidate the skills proper to them, are guided in one way or another by Aristotelian principles in their efforts to deal with contemporary art. I have already mentioned Maritain's basic work, in which he relates the farthest reaches of modern poetry to the little human center of Greek Realism. Mr. Kenneth Burke also, in a very different way, is making an impressive effort to bring this wisdom to bear in our time.

Mr. Burke's theory of "literature as symbolic action" is basically Aristotelian. And from time to time he will give us a reading of a play or a poem in the light of these principles which enables us to see through its language to the life which informs it and gives it its general and perennial significance. But his most sustained work is not criticism, but the analysis of language. He studies language not only as the poet's medium, but as the human medium par excellence. He is not interested in the dead artifacts of language, like the strictly historic scholar, nor is he limited by the up-to-date epistemology and scientific creed of most semanticists. His inspiration, as he has explained himself, is like that of the classic comic dramatist. He contemplates the word-, concept- and symbol-using animal with smiling detachment, and shows him caught in the complexities of his own medium: seduced by its magic and disingenuous glibness, revealing more than he is aware of himself. Mr. Burke's analysis of language itself works like a farcical plot: it is a perpetual-motion machine, or jungle gym for exercising and deflating the literary mind. One reaches the end of a Burkean analysis spent and breathless, but a somewhat better man, and a more forewarned reader of literature.

I have mentioned some of the work which I think basic in the contemporary cult of Humane Letters. I have learned from it as much as I could; but of course in the actual practice of criticism one must rely on one's own acquired habits. My own were formed during many years of directing plays, and I tend to think of the critic's primary task, the "reading" of the novel or play upon which everything must be based, as closely analogous to the "reading" which a performer gives of a piece of music or a dramatic role. The critic holds a ghostly rehearsal for his audience of one, the postulated reader. I like to think of the critic and his silent partner as playing-over the work together, getting the sense of its life and movement, before they talk-it-over in relation to its wider meanings and its relationships to other things.*

But we have a natural desire to see the works of literature we like in relation to each other and to the

* The notion of the performer's talent, especially as it underlies all drama, is further explored in my *The Idea of a Theater*, Princeton University Press, 1949, Anchor Books, 1953.

landmarks of the past. We should like to get our bearings, to satisfy the mind also, as far as that is possible when dealing with a notorious mystery. When Eliot remarked that the artist needs to be able to see how "the whole of the literature of Europe from Homer and within it the whole of the literature of his own country has a simultaneous existence and composes a simultaneous order," he expressed the need which all who are interested in Humane Letters must feel. That is why his famous counsel of perfection has had so wide and beneficent an influence in contemporary literary studies; it reminds us of a basic motive.

I do not know whether Eliot was thinking specifically of Dante when he wrote the early essays in which his critical creed and method are outlined. But I am sure that Dante, more than anyone else in our tradition, attained the understanding of literature as both temporal and perennial, both local and universal, which Eliot demands. This gives Dante a unique value as a historic landmark, and, more intimately, as master of those analogical modes of thought which the artist must use in composing his work, and the critic in seeking significant relationships among the works of the imagination which sprout, in so many forms, out of the changing life of the tradition. For in the *Divine Comedy*, especially the *Purgatory*, one can make out, among other things, Dante's ordered vision of literature. It accommodates all the kinds of *poetando* current in his time, and all those he knew from the past, from the most primitive Greek tales to the most sophisticated works of Ovid and Vergil. They all speak, as though in an endlessly developing dialogue; but Dante does not lose thereby his sense of the pastness of the past. He knew that literature has its historic meaning, the sign of its mortality and its place in the stream of time, as well as its timeless "moral reference" and its "anagoge"—its relation to the ultimate goal of life, itself conceived in so many more or less inadequate ways. In presenting this order Dante does not sacrifice the unique individuality of the poets and their work, and in that lies one of his greatest values for us. When we try to understand the literary tradition we are likely to come out with the history of ideas; but Dante stays within literature by sticking to analogy. His whole method is rooted in analogy; he handled that tool with more skill and sophistication than we do. And it is this lore which the contemporary critic needs, I think, if he is to respect the analogical nature of poetic form, and seek, in his own writing, the analogical kind of understanding proper to literature.*

I do not need to point out that Dante, like Aristotle, is past as well as potentially present. He may at first sight look even more remote, for the languages of the Middle Ages seem queerer than Aristotle's naturalism. But his value for us is similar, and perhaps greater: he returned to the Greek root, rethinking the already ancient conceptions, refining upon them, and above all criticizing and extending them through his own very un-Greek sense of history.

Dante alone does not avail to show us a comprehensive order in the literary tradition as it reaches us—nor, so far as I know, does anything else. The ancient art seems to crop up, in our time, in countless variegated forms, like shoots from an old tree long since grown dead and hollow in the middle. This effect may be due to the fact that a genius with the requisite insight has not yet arrived, to show us a central life. But in bad moments we suspect that even if one of the founding fathers could return to earth to contemplate his progeny he would feel like the Fool's hedge sparrow, who had unknowingly nourished a gigantic and alien cuckoo: "It had it head bit off by it young." And the moral, we fear, would apply also: "So, out went the candle, and we were left darkling."

* Cf. my *Dante's Drama of the Mind: A Modern Reading of the "Purgatorio,"* Princeton University Press, 1953.

We do not blame the poets, playwrights and novelists for the confusion of the modern world. We no longer believe that the poets are the unacknowledged legislators of the race; we do not know whom to accuse. We do not demand that the writer show us an order in the tradition as it reaches us, for order may be lost. We hold a poet responsible only for what he really and intimately sees, and are duly grateful for such harmonies as he does make, limited as they are by what he can hear where he sits, and by what his own sensibility can catch.

Hence the *raison d'être* of a collection of separate essays on modern literature and the theater. The authentic life of Humane Letters is to be found, now, in the diverse achievements of individual artists rather than in any common, central vision. Each modern master grows to maturity in his own unique way from the ancient roots: from the life of Literature itself, which is incarnate in so many arts and languages, and from the instinctive need for an ordered vision of human nature and destiny. All literature exists in the tension between what we naturally need and what we get; modern writers reflect it in countless ways. And the critic, lending ear to the artists as they lend ear to modern experience, must accept it too: he must recognize both his instinctive need for an over-all order, and the multitude of divers strange and beautiful forms in which, in fact, man is reflected in modern art.

CONTENTS

PART I

The Modern Theater

REFLECTIONS ON THE LIFE
OF THE AMERICAN THEATER

Prolegomena

WE are accustomed to take the existence of an American theater for granted, when we think about it at all. That is partly a habit which we formed in the early twenties, when a new and more ambitious generation of theater artists appeared, and partly the result of European interest. When the Londoners flock to our musicals, or the French are stimulated by *A Streetcar Named Desire*, or the Germans adore *Our Town*, it looks as though they were recognizing some new and distinctively American quality.

But on this side of the Atlantic, in the middle fifties, it is not so easy to see what this American quality is— what, for instance, Messrs. Rodgers and Hammerstein, Thornton Wilder, and Tennessee Williams have in common. If there is a common inspiration, or taste, or sense of direction which guides our playwrights, it has never (so far as I know) been elucidated. What seemed to be American playwriting twenty years ago says little to us now, and our great are without progeny. We have, of course, no permanent theatrical establishment; and if there is an "American Theater" in some other sense, it has never been identified critically or historically.

A great deal of information is available on our best-known actors and playwrights. There are a few good, but little-known, accounts of movements in our theater, by Macgowan, Houghton, Clurman, Davis and others, and comments by individuals like Stark Young and Robert Edmond Jones. But the thoughtful studies are obscured by the hullabaloo of the press agents: we treat the theater as essentially impermanent, and it seldom commands the interest of historians, literary men, or students of society. It is significant that O'Neill's posthumous play *Long Day's Journey into Night* was produced in Sweden, to the accompaniment of great interest and critical attention, before it was known here at all. Our theater forgets yesterday's great, and it exists in carefully fostered isolation from the intellectual life of the country.

It seems appropriate, therefore, to raise a few general questions about the life of the American theater, and that is what I wish to attempt in what follows. What has become of the enthusiastic movements and the famous artists who used to represent our theater? What position does the theater occupy in our society? How is the art supported? What social, economic and cultural forces govern its precarious life?

Such an enquiry, even if one knew enough to carry it out completely, could hardly throw much light directly upon the art of the theater. But in the present state of our theatrical culture it is a necessary preliminary. The comedy or tragedy of our theater's struggle for life is perhaps of more significance than the plays themselves. And if we are to do justice to the achievements as well as the frustrations of our theater artists we must try to understand the wider scene in which they cultivate their art.

The American Theater Between the Wars

I

THE ill-defined notion of "The American Theater" first
became current about the end of World War I, with
the beginnings of the old Provincetown Players. There
had been some self-consciously American playwriting as
early as the Revolution, and all through the nineteenth
century we had barnstorming companies playing Shakespeare and melodrama; touring stars from England or
the Continent, native popular forms of vaudeville, and
later the Minstrel Shows. But on the whole we were
content to leave the theater to Europeans and to the
special tribe of show-people, until the Little Theater
movement reached us from England and Ireland, in-
spiring us with more ambitious ideas. Our Little Theater
movement was part of a general ferment, a somewhat
naive effort (as it looks in retrospect) to do for Manchester or Dublin or Chicago what the Comédie Française does for Paris.

New movements in our theater always begin in more
or less explicit opposition to the taste, the standards and
the working conditions of the entertainment industry.
The Little Theater movement sought an alternative to
Broadway and all it stands for; so did the socially conscious theaters of the thirties, and so does the present

"off-Broadway" movement. The history of our theater for the last forty years may be understood as a succession of non-commercial theaters which failed, but in failing provided a much-needed shot in the arm—new artists, new ideas, new plays—for the strictly commercial theater which we have always with us.

The main outlines of this often-repeated pattern have been clear for some time to all interested observers of the theater. The late Edith J. R. Isaacs, who was for many years the editor of *Theatre Arts Monthly*, began to make it out in the middle twenties, and she offered an interpretation of it which is still the best attempt to make sense of this little piece of social or cultural history. It was she who distinguished the "tributary theater" from the "real" or "professional theater," which we associate with Broadway and its gigantic suburbs in Hollywood, the radio, and TV. By "tributary theater" she meant primarily the little (or "art") theaters which then dotted the country. She was inclined to include also the more famous groups in New York: the Provincetown, the Neighborhood Playhouse, the Laboratory Theatre, and others which existed then and later. She had in mind community theaters like the Cleveland Playhouse, and such pioneer academic theaters as George Pierce Baker's projects at Harvard and Yale. She saw even then that the tributary theaters found it difficult to survive against the all-pervasive power and influence of the entertainment industry. But the atmosphere of that time was joyful; we were supposed to be in the midst of a fundamental renaissance of the theater: "the great American play" and "the great American theater," we were sure, were just around the corner. In accordance with this bullish spirit Mrs. Isaacs assumed that Broadway itself was getting the new religion, and she assigned an honorable, if subsidiary, role to the tributary theater also. She thought its function was to promote interest in the theater in the provinces and suburbs, and to give young artists their start. Broadway would select the best of these, and in the severer atmosphere of Times Square (as she thought of it) bring them at last to their artistic maturity. Hence her metaphor for the pattern of the theater's life: the little theaters and the repertory theaters, the academic and community theaters, were to be thought of as tiny streams rising in the Bronx or the Dakotas, then humbly pouring their little contributions into the Father of Waters, Broadway itself. And there—between Fortieth and Fifty-second—the longed-for American Theater would arise.

Mrs. Isaacs saw the essential pattern with remarkable clarity, considering the time in which she wrote. She saw how the theater's struggle for life perpetually begins —what might be called the first act of the tearful comedy. But now—thirty years later—we are in a better position than she was to understand the turning point of the second act, when the embattled actor or playwright comes to terms with the entertainment industry, and the somewhat bathetic finale when the tributary theater dries up completely and Broadway is still Broadway, just as before. Moreover, having lived through the Great Depression and another war, we can see more clearly than she could how dependent the theater is upon the changing moods of the country as a whole. The theater's struggle for life could only be understood completely if we could see it against the background of those climactic events, and those currents in political, economic and intellectual life, which make the history of our changing society.

There were two main movements in our theater between the wars: the Little Theater movement, which did not survive the crash of '29, and the "socially conscious" theaters of the thirties which faded away with the approach of World War II. It was the Little Theater movement which initiated the sequence of renaissances the latest of which is the present off-Broadway movement.

The immediate impulse of the Little Theater movement came to us from England and Ireland, but before long we began to look beyond Manchester or Dublin to the great repertory theaters of the Continent. Copeau, the Moscow Art Theatre, Reinhardt, Grasso, the Chauve Souris, the ballet, visited this country, and our young people of the theater went abroad to study with the masters. The long procession of refugee theater artists began coming from Europe. Among the earliest and most important of these were Richard Boleslavsky and Maria Ouspenskaya, who introduced so many Americans to the strict and suggestive techniques of the Moscow Art Theatre; but there have been many others. Both in its beginnings and for several years thereafter the Little Theater movement took its cue from Europe; the brilliant repertory theaters of the Continent suddenly revealed to a new generation what the theater might be at its best. The leaders of the movement envied the beautifully trained companies to be seen abroad; the repertories including the best plays of every style and period; the studios, the devoted audiences, and the enlightened critical attention which the theater enjoyed in France and Germany. It was argued that we ought to have such theaters in this country, enjoying the same sort of intelligent support as music and painting enjoy. And to distinguish theaters of this kind from show business the Little Theater movement adopted as its slogan the fighting word "Art."

After thirty years this program still seems natural enough. It is not hard to understand the fervor, intelligence, talent and devotion which, in fact, it commanded —nor, in retrospect, its touching innocence. The leaders of the movement did not fully understand how long it had taken to produce the theatrical culture they admired in Europe, nor how difficult it would be to create an analogous American theater. Some of the farcical aspects of their efforts are caught in George Kelly's *The Torch-Bearers,* a comedy about a little theater group which is determined to bring Art to Main Street whether Main Street likes it or not.

By the late twenties, the time of the Big Money, as Dos Passos called it, the Little Theater movement was growing bewildered and discouraged. The crash of twenty-nine, after which no one had any money for Art, proved to be the death blow. Some of the refugees started tearooms or interior-decorating shops; some started teaching; and some were bought up, piecemeal, as marketable commodities, by the entertainment industry. When Mr. Norris Houghton toured the country in the thirties, to see what had become of the theaters celebrated in Kenneth MacGowan's *Footlights Across America,* he found some of the theaters, but little of the life, of the original movement. But it had performed the task assigned to the tributary theater by Mrs. Isaacs: it had fed our theatrical life with new artists and new ideas. Some of its leaders—O'Neill, Paul Green, Robert Edmond Jones, Stark Young, for example—represent the best of what we call the American theater. Some of its ideas (the technique of the Moscow Art Theatre, modern stage design out of Appia and Gordon Craig) still have their beneficent influence. Though the hope which inspired it, the hope of a permanent theater outside show business, now looks as quaint as the picture of one's dead grandmother, it certainly was a source of new life, exactly according to the first part of Mrs. Isaacs' scheme.

The second tributary theater movement (during the decade of the thirties) was the heir, and in some respects a resumption, of the Little Theater movement, both in its personnel and in its aims. Harold Clurman, of the Group Theatre, had worked at the Neighborhood Playhouse and the Laboratory Theatre. Hallie Flanagan Davis, of the Federal Theatre, was a veteran of the academic theaters. This movement also sought an alternative to Broadway: audiences, interest and support quite outside the strictly commercial theater. But the driving force behind it was new; its watchword was "society" rather than "art." The Federal Theatre and the Group Theatre epitomize the two most important aspects of this "socially conscious" movement.

The Federal Theatre was of course a direct creation of the Roosevelt regime. It was ostensibly a relief project, but under Mrs. Davis it became, in fact, much more than that, as one can see by reading her history of its life, *Arena*. Mrs. Davis quotes in her book this statement of the initial aims of the Federal Theatre: "To set up theaters which have the possibilities of growing into social institutions in the communities in which they are located and thus to provide future employment for at least some of those who now present an immediate and acute problem to the government . . . and to lay the foundation for the development of a truly creative theater in the United States with outstanding producing centers in each of those regions which have common interests as a result of geography, language origins, history, tradition, customs of the people." This statement could only have been written by one (presumably Mrs. Davis) who had digested the experience of the Little Theater movement, and wished to promote its essential aims in the light of that experience. She knew that the little theaters had briefly flourished in various parts of the country, with their varied racial, cultural and regional traditions. Her plan, in direct opposition to the colorless uniformity of mass entertainment, was democratic in the best sense of the word: she wanted to recognize the *various* elements in our complex society, and also the various versions of the theatrical art itself which had excited the little theaters in their day. Under her leadership every kind of theater artist, refugees both from the show shops and the little theaters, emerged from hiding and went to work for the Federal Theatre. Every kind of play, from Agitprop to T. S. Eliot, from Aeschylus to Marc Blitzstein, lighted the barns, the lofts, and the darkened commercial theaters of the depression period. And, most significant of all, new audiences for this new kind of theater suddenly assembled all over the country.

The life of the Federal Theatre was brief: from the fall of 1935 to June 30, 1939. In that short time it could not, of course, realize any of its statesmanlike aims of giving the theater a recognized and stable place in our complex and shifting society. It worked in haste, under the pressure of real misery, improvising its organization and its methods as it went along. Many of its productions showed all too clearly the signs of the chaos in which they had been put together. But the best of them had a style which triumphantly accepted the precarious situation, an immediate and headlong vitality which I will never forget. This excitement, which is so rare in our theater—the ancient magic of "two boards and a passion"—was obviously the joint creation of the performers, the theater-hungry audiences, and the amazing patronage of the government, which for once gave the theater a status and an interest entirely unlike that of the show shops. The Federal Theatre was thus a unique demonstration of what the theatrical life of the country might be. The monopoly of Broadway was broken; the country was in one of its crusading moods, questioning everything; and the Federal Theatre provided, however feverishly, the public discussion of ideas, the shared images of human life, which the theater shows when it is alive. It is doubtful whether the Federal Theatre could have survived, even if Congress had not murdered it, for by 1939 the approach of war was restoring "normalcy." But it lasted long enough to give us a fleeting glimpse of that "theater" which the torch-bearers of the Little Theaters and their heirs have always dreamed of.

The Group Theatre, whose life coincides with the thirties, was as significant as the Federal Theatre, but for nearly opposite reasons. The Federal Theatre provided plenty of new artists, plays and ideas; but it was its statesmanlike plans, and its experimental demonstration of the possibility of a non-commercial theater, which gave it its unique importance. The Group Theatre on the other hand was a tightly-knit company of young artists, and what they did was to make the best theater, complete with acting ensemble, directors, playwrights, and audience, which we have ever had. The Federal Theatre came and went as government support was provided and withdrawn, while the Group, emerging from the streets of New York, lived from hand to mouth on the edge of the market, improvising its financing and its philosophy as it went along.

The story of the Group Theatre is told in Harold Clurman's book, *The Fervent Years*, a document of great value for the social historian as well as for the student of the theater. The relation of the Group to its predecessors in the Little Theater movement is suggested in an anecdote which Mr. Clurman tells in his book. Stark Young's *The Saint* was being produced, in the late twenties, by O'Neill, Robert Edmond Jones, and Macgowan, three leaders of that early movement. Clurman, then a very young man, was present, and heard a talk that Jones gave to the company. I quote from Mr. Clurman's book (page 8): "'The theater is a dream that the audience comes to behold,'" Mr. Clurman reports Jones as saying. "'The theater is revelation. I look about me here, and I do not see light, I do not perceive dream, I do not feel revelation. That is what I wanted to tell you, Mary, Charlie, Norma——' He walked up the aisle and disappeared. Macgowan asked Gene if he had anything to add. Gene indicated that he didn't. There was a tense pause. That was all. The actors got up and left." Mr. Clurman continues: "I was rather touched by Bobby Jones's speech. Jones was an artist, one of the very few in the American theater. Yet I realized immediately that he had made no connection with his actors. . . . It seemed to me to be Jones's fault that he was not understood. It was the leader's task to fashion a common language and a common point of reference with those whom he hoped to lead."

12

In that episode the inspiration of the Little Theater movement, its artist's creed, and its eventual helplessness are clear, and also the new sense of direction represented by the Group: the new emphasis upon "society" in every sense. Mr. Clurman and his associates devoted themselves precisely to the task he mentioned: fashioning a common language and a common point of reference. The common language they found for the theater itself was the technical vocabulary of the Moscow Art Theatre, as derived from the teachings of Boleslavsky and Ouspenskaya. The "common point of reference" turned out to be that burning interest in the immediate American scene which the whole country shared in the early and middle thirties. It was that which gave the Group a sufficient (if vague) ideological coherence; and it was that which provided it with a devoted audience and a sanction or recognition beyond that of the entertainment industry. During its nine years of life the Group devoted itself entirely to contemporary American plays, and it developed several new playwrights of its own, of whom Clifford Odets was the most talented and accomplished.

The Moscow Art Theatre techniques, as adapted by the Group, continue to be cultivated by many of our best actors, when they can find the time; some of the Group's plays have, perhaps, permanent value; and artists of various kinds who learned their art in the Group account for many of the better things on Broadway. But the Group itself disbanded in 1939, not for lack of "success," but (as Mr. Clurman explains) because they felt that the social sanction which had unified them and given them their recognized place had leaked away.

The history of our theater between the wars, if one considers it in such broad terms as I have suggested, confirms Mrs. Isaacs' notion that the sources of our theater's life are mainly in the recurrent tributary theaters. But it is now evident that the golden moment when the theater artist makes the grade on Broadway does not come off as happily as she thought it would. The essential structure of Broadway, with its peculiar mind and taste, changes far less than the artists who are compelled to come to terms with it. Many of the artists themselves have explained the artistic frustrations of show business; they like its rewards, the swimming pools, the Jaguars, all that goes with success, but they must look elsewhere for their nourishment as artists. They may collect modern French paintings, or flirt with the party line, or start little theaters in the suburbs of Hollywood, or sneak off to the Brattle Theatre to play Pirandello or to Fourth Street to play Chekhov—but very little of their intellectual and artistic impulses can be satisfied on Broadway. And the notion of a real theater continues to hover over the scene, with the guilty air of unfinished business, or the regretful air of lost illusions.

Moreover we now see, as Mrs. Isaacs could not, that there is a last act in the endlessly repeated drama, or comedy, of our theater's struggle for life. The final act is played out when the Broadway product is exported. Broadway may originate little, but it puts its mark on everything it buys and sells—the sleek, packaged look of the world's richest market. And when this product reaches the suburbs and the provinces, in warmed-over productions, as a Broadway star in last year's "vehicle," in further dilution for Hollywood, radio or TV, it stands for *the* theater wherever it goes. The hard-pressed director of a small theater in Nashville or Urbana (or, for that matter, Paris or Milan) finds that his original production of a new play by a little-known local author is in direct competition with the packaged product. He knows that his audiences have been "conditioned" by the all-pervasive power of national advertising to demand the Broadway certificate, and like it, while no one has told them what to make of *his* homemade show. He may continue for years, if he has the stamina, to consult his own taste and try to build the taste of his audience, but, if so, he is barely holding his own against the tide.

At a certain point he will shrug his shoulders and become a distributor of the nationally advertised product: a "Grade B" summer stock company by arrangement with Equity and the stagehands' unions, or a five-year-old Broadway play, by arrangement with the Authors' Guild. By this simple device he can be sure of making twice the money at a tenth of the effort. And so Mrs. Isaacs' tributary streams dry up, and the much-used waters they contributed to the entertainment industry back up, drowning everything once more, in the same stale flood.

II

The hectic life of our theater between the wars is somewhat mysterious, like all real history, especially to anyone who was connected with it. A theater, even a single good production, is an intense experience for the participants while it lasts, but when it is over it is gone completely. There is hardly time, in the rush of our lives, even to remember it. Perhaps that is one reason why the enquirer has so little to go on: the memory of our "theater" is insanely short; the experience of the last thirty or forty years has not been digested.

I suppose we must wait until the longed-for critical and historical sense appears in our theater—a common taste and sense of direction—before we can hope to make sense out of its struggles. When the American theater is built we shall be able to write the epic of its rise. But in the meantime we may try to see why both the Little Theater movement and the more socially conscious theaters of the thirties disappeared so swiftly and completely. In general, it looks as though both the "inspiration" of those movements themselves and the social sanction which gave them their lease on life in the community were in essence short-lived, too superficial to last.

The Little Theater movement was the creation of

comparatively well-to-do, cultivated—not to say "genteel"—Americans; people who were socially secure at home and knew Europe. It was related to that wider reform movement which we associate with "gentlemen in politics"; Theodore Roosevelt in some of his moods, and of course Wilson, with his New Freedom. The country was tired of its debauch of money-making, which had lasted since the end of the Civil War, discouraging so many intelligent Americans with all forms of public life, whether in art or politics. Political leaders of this new type tried to work out for themselves responsible, disinterested careers of public service; and in this effort they often looked abroad, especially to England, with its more stable tradition, for guidance and encouragement. In a closely analogous way, the leaders of the Little Theater movement looked to the European theaters as their models; and they too were sustained by the reforming spirit of the times. All over the country people from the right side of the railroad tracks were setting forth to provide light and leading. The face of the Little Theater movement is the face of Woodrow Wilson himself; it has the fine intellectual features above the hard collar, the intently glittering pince-nez, of the gently reared American girding himself for a crusade.

We know how this whole reform movement ended, when business boomed to more fabulous heights, and the country shrugged off its crusading mood, returning to the more familiar and congenial notion of public life as a racket. The disappearance of the public sanction which the reform movement had provided would be enough to account for the collapse of the little theaters. But I am afraid that their inspiration had run out anyway.

They had been inspired by the theatrical life of Europe; but the European theaters were the expression of an old, eclectic, perhaps decadent culture. They were not themselves building a form of drama adequate to the modern world, but rather reflecting, in sophisticated productions, innumerable contemporary isms and innumerable memories of past glories. Europe could show us (like a very cultivated old man mulling over his past reading, playing with half-ironic subtleties of interpretation) the exciting possibilities of the art in general. But it could not show us the drama of our time, especially as it occurs in this country.

The inspiration we got from Europe in the early twenties was not enough to create an American theater, but we must remember that it did suffice to nourish a number of interesting individual talents. Stark Young's sensitive feeling for the arts of the theater, especially as expressed in his critical writings, was developed by a familiarity with the best in Europe. One can see that Robert Edmond Jones was a sort of lyric poet of design, as good as the best Europeans; if he was somewhat thwarted in the long run, it was because, in show business, he was so often compelled to spend his talents on third-rate material. O'Neill must be understood as a "post-Ibsen" playwright. He is more akin to Strindberg, Andreyev, Pirandello, than to anything in this country. Perhaps the harsh, dead quality of his language (of which various observers have complained) is due to the fact that he found so few conscious American embodiments of the themes derived from contemporary Europe: hence his abstractness and his violence, both signs of frustration. Yet he did what he could, in this country, to live the life of modern drama after Ibsen.

The other arts in this country, music, painting, and poetry, were waking up under European influences at the same time. But they fared better than the theater. Poetry found enough sustenance in the little magazines to live on; and though the audience for American poetry remains small, that art has attained a high level of accomplishment with us. But the theater cannot be cultivated in solitude, in the time the artist can save from his regular job. A group art from the very beginning, it depends upon a certain community of feeling and aim;

and it was in this respect that the "inspiration" derived from Europe proved inadequate. The torch-bearers of our first theatrical awakening could not build together; they lacked a common language and a common point of reference, as Mr. Clurman put it in the passage I quoted from his book.

This dictum would have to be modified a bit in the case of our regional drama. The clue to regional drama came from Europe too, and for a time we thought that rocky New England or the rural South might develop theaters on the analogy of Yeats's labors in Ireland. The work of Paul Green, Lynn Riggs, and the early O'Neill reflect this influence. The best of our regional dramas are as good as anything we have done, and yet there is something artificial about that school. O'Neill's meager farm kitchens were more popular in Greenwich Village than in Maine; the home folks might make good copy, but they did not, on the whole, accept the dramatists' pictures of themselves. There is, I think, some life left in our regional traditions, but the forces of our industrial society and our national melting pot weaken it rapidly. We preserve the local flavor for its tourist appeal, encouraging the New Englanders to turn their white houses into motels, and the Navahos to sell blankets at the railroad stations on the Santa Fe. The predestined end of our regional drama is figured in the sequence which proceeds from Oklahoma to New York, and then from *Green Grow the Lilacs* to the Broadway musical *Oklahoma!* and, at last, the movie version.

The Little Theater movement was akin in many respects to Wilsonian idealism, and, like it, proved incapable of surviving to maturity. The socially conscious theaters of the thirties are similarly related to the New Deal. Samuel Lubell, in his *Future of American Politics*, has made an illuminating study of the "Roosevelt Revolution," in which he identifies the elements in our society that made it, and the half-conscious motive that gave it some coherence. After a careful study of the voting in the Roosevelt victories he concludes that they were made by "the children of the 13,000,000 immigrants who poured into this country between 1900 and 1914." Their motive, sharpened by the crash of '29, was to complete their climb from the immigrant status into the respectable American middle class. This they accomplished with great rapidity under the leadership of the Roosevelt regime; and by the end of the thirties, as war and prosperity returned, the mild revolution was practically complete. Now we are all in the same boat—or the same hastily built suburb—wondering, in the intervals of the race for money, what to do next. It is surprising how accurately Henry James foresaw this drama fifty years ago, when he speculated on the fate of the new and still-growing immigrant population, and recorded his observations and his hunches in *The American Scene*.

The Federal Theatre under Mrs. Davis reflects the leadership of this movement in its most enlightened aspect, and also its pragmatic, improvised quality: one thinks of it, not as an idealistic gentleman, but a sweating committeeman in shirt sleeves, armed with a volume of Freud, a volume of Marx, and several filing cabinets full of statistics.

The Group Theatre apparently owed its being, not directly to the Roosevelt regime, but to the "revolutionary" movement that put Roosevelt in power. The plays which Clifford Odets wrote for the Group during the decade of the thirties, from *Waiting for Lefty* and *Awake and Sing!* through *Paradise Lost* and *Rocket to the Moon* to *Golden Boy*, reveal in various lights the forces driving the new recruits to our middle class: the violent appetite for racing cars and two-toned Oxfords; the disarming soul-searching; the flirtation with Marxism; the final loss of purpose as the "revolution" ends and prosperity returns. There can be no doubt of the genuineness of Odets's inspiration in these plays; he is the poet of a class in our society and a moment of history. But the tale he had to tell was soon ended, and he was so close to it, as it unfolded, that he could not see it in any perspective. The vaguely Marxian moral which he tacks on to his early plays does not really apply to the story he has to tell. The currency of Marxian ideas in the thirties merely shows that we had no conception of history of our own, no philosophy of man and his society, to help us get our bearings in the crises of the times.

The Group Theatre nourished many fine artists besides Odets, but his plays show, with special clarity, the limitations as well as the authenticity of the Group's "inspiration." The focus upon immediate experience, both in its realistic version of the Moscow Art Theatre's acting technique and in its direct reflection of the current scene and current issues, made the vitality of the Group; but when the immediate scene changed at the end of the thirties, that life was gone. The Group did not last long enough to produce any play except contemporary American work—it could not even begin to relate its art to the great tradition we share with Europe. And (another sign of the same failing) it could not understand its themes in relation to our own history. It had the disarming quality of adolescence, when every experience seems absolutely unique—as intense, suggestive, and undigested as a dream.

The relationships between the life of our theater and the life of our politics have not yet, so far as I know, been studied in detail. But even the few observations I have made suggest that further study would be illuminating. The art of the theater—notoriously an "impure" art—seems to be as close to the art of politics as it is to poetry, painting or music. The theater artist, whether actor or playwright, depends upon the interest and support of an audience, just as the politician depends upon his constituency. The politician cannot practice his art at all without a grant from his constituency; and so he must first of all woo *it*. And the theater artist cannot practice his art without real people assembled before a real stage; a theater without an audience is a contradiction in terms. That is why both politics and the theater are necessarily so close to the public mood and the public mind of their times.

In politics we recognize a distinction between the "practical politician" who is interested solely in getting and keeping political power, and the statesman, who must have political power too, but uses it in the service of a philosophy of government. The practical politician is only a creature of his times; the statesman, while in the thick of the temporal struggle, tries to build something permanent. When we discuss the theater we usually do not make a distinction of this kind; we tend to assume that it can only live from hand to mouth, ceasing to exist the moment the curtain goes down on the last performance. But the theoretical possibility of statesmanship in the theater, and of a theater which establishes something lasting in its own country, does exist. One could say, I think, that Corneille, Racine and Molière built a lasting "theater" for modern France—by which I mean not only the Comédie Française itself, but a common conception of the theater which is at once alive in France and consciously related to the tradition in other countries and in the past. It is this which guides and nourishes theater artists in France still, and gives them a recognized place in the life of their country. The creative generations in the middle of the seventeenth century did for the French theater something like what the makers of the Constitution did for our politics, when they set up a system of government for eighteenth-century America, in the light of the best political thought of that time and of the past. These instances remind one that creative moments in either art—when statesmanship as distinguished from timeserving or frantic improvisation is possible—are rare and unpredictable. But if we are to get any perspective on our own times, any understanding of the accomplishments and the failures of our contemporaries, it is the great moments we must remember.

With this in mind, it appears that very little fundamental construction was possible in this country between the wars, whether in the theater or in politics. In politics, reform movements have come and gone with bewildering rapidity. In the theater many talents and many movements have briefly flourished. There has been no dearth of intelligent, devoted and high-minded figures, who have done what they could to exploit their moments of power and recognition for creative ends. But most of this excitement is already beginning to look shallow and myopic. Perhaps the country as a whole obscurely feels that; for the moment one of our crusading moods passes, and "normalcy" supervenes, we are glad to relinquish politics to the full-time practical politicians, and the theater to the professionals of advertising and show business.

Broadway

THE entertainment industry is, of course, not confined to this country. Our plays and films are exported all over the world, and now Europe, and even Japan, contribute their share to the flood of mass entertainment. What makes Broadway unique is that it represents not only commercial entertainment but also *the* theater: in this country no other conception of the theater—of its possible value or meaning, its place in society, or its role in the life of our culture—has ever taken root. Thus we look to Broadway to provide our equivalent of Sophocles and Molière, and at the same time judge it (along with the night clubs) as a going concern in the "luxury" field.

Everyone knows Broadway, where it glitters, with a more snobbish and expensive glitter, among the movie palaces, flea circuses, and dance halls of midtown Manhattan. It is a part of our folklore, like football week ends and political rallies. Moreover, the structure of Broadway as a business, and the conditions it imposes on its artists, have often been explained. Not much that is new remains to be said about Broadway, but perhaps it is appropriate to assemble the picture again. For Broadway is the most constant element in our theater's life—the "normal" place of that art with us.

The excitement which we associate with Broadway comes less from the shows we see there than from the

heady gamble of *producing* a show. The odds are all
against the producer; as business, Broadway is riskier
than gold bricks or swamplands in Florida. No one
knows, in advance, whether a show will be a hit; but
everyone knows that the initial costs and the running
costs are so high that unless it *is* a hit everyone will lose
a great deal of money, and, what is more dangerous, the
reputation of marketability (in the case of the artists)
and of being able to guess the market (in the case of the
producer). But when a show is a hit the national slot
machine suddenly pours forth its flood of gold, and all
who have been connected with the show are instantly
promoted to the status of "luminous," "compassionate"
and "incandescent" artists of the theater.

This game seems to satisfy the gamblers' instincts of
the angels and producers, and the more guileless appetite for glamour of the Broadway audience; but the cold-
eyed interests that control Broadway do not share in
any of the excitement. Those who can count on making
money are the owners of Broadway real estate; the
unions of stagehands, electricians, scene painters, costume makers, truckers and box-office attendants; and
auxiliary professionals like the press agents and the play
reviewers on the big dailies. These elements all enjoy
monopolies in their various realms, and are thus in a
position to exact their "take" from every show in advance. It is they who make the risk of production so
absurdly high; but they do not themselves take any risk;
they leave that to the producers and their angels, and
to the artists who actually work on the show. It is a
system which guarantees the stability of the monopolis-
tic business and labor interests surrounding Broadway,
and the complete instability of anything which could be
called "theater."

Though nothing in the show shops lasts, a certain
fairly constant atmosphere is generated—recognizable
but indefinable; the pretentious but somewhat guilty atmosphere of show-business-as-theater: the curious es-

sence we know as Broadway. Whatever appears on Times Square has some of this Broadway look, as though the neighborhood itself could confer it, like those infallible acids whereby Hollywood can bleach any young girl, however charming she may be herself, into this year's standard starlet. Sartre's play, *Les Main Sales,* is one thing in the French film, quite another as the Broadway play, *Red Gloves.* The actor who seems quite at home in one of the big money-makers on Times Square may be quite different, two months later, when he sneaks off to play in the Village. Some of the same individuals who constituted the exciting audiences for the Federal Theatre now make up that totally different thing, a Broadway audience. I think, therefore, that the Broadway atmosphere is not due to those who work there, but rather to the stereotyped postures which the show-shop regime forces upon them. If we can't define the mind and taste of Broadway, we may be able to understand something about it by remembering how its producers and its artists are obliged to work.

The producer is a key figure in the Broadway setup. Anyone who has, or can find, the money can be a producer; but those who last in this profession for a few years are obliged to develop the special caginess, the impersonal craftiness, of the market diagnostician. In this job there is very little room for the exercise of personal taste, and the producer renounces that luxury early in his career, unless he happens to be a natural thermometer of the entertainment market, like the fabulous hero of *Once in a Lifetime.* As entrepreneur, he is between the investor (or angel) and the show. But he cannot afford his own acting company, theater, director, designer or musician; his own organization consists of a small office and a skeleton office staff. He shops around for stars with "names," directors and designers with good reputations, orchestrators who have, as nearly as may be, the infallible touch; and out of these elements (often quite strange to each other) he puts together his show.

25

The arts of the producer are thus essentially those of merchandising, and the producer is very much like the buyer in a big department store, or the designer of shop-windows. In New York, the world's richest city, he commands the same resources as the fashion experts and the decorators of Persian night clubs and Tudor tea-rooms. Hence the sleek, expensive, tasteless quality of the typical Broadway success. Everything in it has cost a lot of money, and can subdue the meek herds of patrons with the authority of the market itself.

It is those who actually make the show—directors, actors, designers and the rest—who occupy the most false and impossible position in this system. There are no permanent jobs for them on Broadway, and of course no possibility of learning how to work together, or of developing their own art and their own taste. They are strictly marketable commodities in a buyers' market; no wonder they lose their human flavor so soon, looking less and less like themselves, and more and more like the ads for whisky, perfume, and Caribbean cruises.

We sometimes tend to think that it is the professional playwrights who make Broadway what it is. But if they are to play the game of the entertainment market, they must accept its subtle rules like everyone else: they too must consult the market first, and their own taste and intelligence second. This point was explained with impressive clarity by Mr. Abe Burrows in a recent issue of *The New York Times'* Sunday Theatre Page. "Playwrights," he says, "are the products of their culture. They reflect every strength and weakness of the culture, both as artists and as human beings. This is a confused age we live in and the dramas depicting it are bound to be just as confused. This is an age that equates value with success. In fact, it values only success and, in turn, success is largely measured in terms of money. In striving for this monetary success, all of us are scrambling in a huge market place. Our playwrights are right smack in the middle of that market place, too. And that

26

is a deadly spot for a man who is trying to give some insight into his world."

It is the critics on the daily papers who render the first verdict of failure or "success." For this reason the daily-reviewer is more feared and cursed one minute, and worshiped with more tearful gratitude the next, than anything on Broadway except the box office itself. But it is, I think, as unrealistic to blame the (often good-hearted) individual reviewers as it is to blame the playwrights. The job itself of daily-reviewing is an integral part of the Broadway system, and as such is surrounded with so many subtle taboos that the occupant of the job has little chance to develop an intelligible point of view of his own. The critics on the weeklies are much freer to consult their own taste; it is to them that we must look for "criticism" in the usual sense of the word.

The job of daily-reviewer is firmly based on the mystery of Broadway itself: the paradox of show business as theater. Thus, the reviewer in his aisle seat represents the hoped-for customer, like the buyer at a fashion show. He is called upon to exercise some choice among the products hopefully displayed; but he knows that his reputation as market diagnostician is at stake—that the excellent trade journal *Variety* will publish, in the spring, an analysis of the reports of the daily-reviewers, grading them according to their ability to pick a hit. He also knows that, as part of the entertainment industry, he must do his share to "create" a market. This requirement is clearly suggested in the following rather rueful paragraph by Mr. Walter Kerr of *The Herald Tribune* in *How Not to Write a Play:*

For one reason or another, the contemporary American cannot be persuaded that the legitimate drama is a tolerable form of entertainment. All sorts of persuasions are repeatedly tried. The newspaper reviewers, for instance, flirt with perjury in the nightly effort to make the theater seem gay. One recent Broadway season was, by common consent, the worst in the memory of man.

The plays which went to make up this season were described in the daily press as "stunning," "magnificent," "exuberant," "distinguished," "exhilarating," "enormously enjoyable," "enchanting," "extraordinary," and "filled with wit, talent and splendor." The playgoer remained skeptical.

The daily-reviewer is thus necessarily part of show *business;* but as guardian of the Broadway mystery he must write his verdicts (in about half an hour, around midnight the day the show opens) with the mysterious air of the connoisseur of the arts of the theater. It is perhaps for that reason that he finds such adjectives as Mr. Kerr quotes—encomiums which would make Shakespeare blush—for the lucky show that meets with his approval. And when a play rubs him the wrong way, whether it be by Lorca, Cummings, or Dostoevski, or the stage-struck wife of one of the angels, he damns it utterly, as though he spoke for the theater in general— or as though his sense of the Broadway market gave him the authority to decide whether any play was "theater" at all.

Mr. Kerr's remarks suggest that the daily-reviewers cannot create a hit. For a show to be a hit—i.e., make money—it must run for two months, or, if it is a big musical, for eight or ten months at least; and no form of promotion can guarantee that. But the reviewers do have the power to kill a show, because most theatergoers look at their reports when deciding where to go. There are few if any instances of a show which has survived the disapproval of the daily-reviewers, even when enthusiastically supported by the producer, the critics on the weeklies, and interested members of the audience. The daily-reviewer is thus an important part of the mechanism whereby the Broadway taste or atmosphere is maintained: he can exile to outer darkness the many kinds of theater which are not "Broadway."

Mr. Burrows, in the article from which I have quoted, suggests some of the reasons why we look to "success measured largely in terms of money" to decide all questions of value. Our age, as he says, is confused; which means, I take it, that we do not know what forms of life or art to choose. As individuals we may be guided by habits, tastes and ideas derived from our own experience, and from the particular regional or racial or religious tradition in which we were brought up. But in public we do not express this taste. We know that all traditions lose most of their meaning in the national scene, and that the little-understood forces of our industrial society are changing the scene with increasing speed. It is natural, at this bewildered moment, to let the market rule, for its pronouncements are as impersonal and as mathematically accurate as those of a Geiger counter. And they carry great authority; for unless a man can "meet a market" he may fail, undernourished both physically and spiritually, while meeting a market may bring fabulous wealth. The market seems to know what forms of life and art are destined to survive in our society. It is easier to trust it—out of timidity, respect for money, and hopeful good will—than to attempt moral or esthetic judgments of one's own.

It is, of course, the media of mass entertainment and mass advertising which present the human image with the widest public acceptance. Those who confect the shows, the commercials, and the advertisements which absorb millions of listeners, viewers and magazine readers twenty-four hours a day appear to follow the principle expressed by Sabina in Mr. Thornton Wilder's *The Skin of Our Teeth:* "I don't think the theater is a place where people's feelings ought to be hurt," she says. Her sentiment is friendly; it is easy to recognize in it our inarticulate need for some cozy realm of the spirit where we might all be the same nice people together. Our faith in the market is sustained by a flabby version of our faith in democracy itself, and the taboos which surround the mass media, ruling out all reference to differences among us, whether regional or racial or religious, or even of age—for all grandmothers are as spry as maidens by this rule, as they sprint out to the backyard to hang up the wash, or pull a pie from the oven with an inanely brilliant grin—reveal perhaps, not only our techniques for seducing the consumer, but an element of tender democratic delicacy. But the mass media, when thus strictly limited, are impervious to most of the actualities of human life: they make that "non-conducting atmosphere" which Henry James mentioned. Backed by the authority of our gravest industrialists, the weight of vast wealth, and the magic of applied science, the image of *Homo Americanus* which flickers on a million screens and is murmured simultaneously into a million ears is of unbearable silliness, like the childishness of senility.

As market, Broadway belongs in the comparatively small "luxury" class, and the vision of human life which it projects is more like that of the "after-shave club" than that of the ads, in family magazines, for trusses or detergents. Its initial appeal is snobbish—to those who can afford it. But the ideal of universal marketability exercises a strong and ever-increasing pressure upon it. Hollywood began as a distended suburb of Broadway, but now it would be truer to say that Broadway is an uneasy and less and less important suburb of Hollywood, radio and TV. Arrangements for movie and TV rights become the most important part of a Broadway contract, and without the golden hope of the mass market, the afterlife in the mass media, it is doubtful whether Broadway would continue to exist.

I have been endeavoring to describe the general situation of Broadway, and the key figures in the show-shop regime: the producer, the performers, the playwright, and the daily-reviewer, as a way of understanding the flickering life on Times Square: the docility of the paying customer; the falsity which the market regime forces upon even the finest professionals; the artificially hopped-up excitement which accompanies a hit, the irrational violence with which a show felt to be "not

Broadway" is rejected. But the basic paradox of Broadway is that it is not only a show *shop*, but also all we normally have as a theater; and this paradox accounts, I think, both for the frustrations of Broadway artists and for the fact that a more vital kind of theater from time to time crashes through there. The best foreign companies are marketed on Broadway; now and then a production which has succeeded in London will be imported, and work, for a time, as a *succès d'estime*. And every now and then a new artist, performer or playwright who is a "natural," will be put over by a shrewd agent. Our theater artists are obliged to besiege Broadway, and the market itself (as it speaks in box-office figures, "success measured in money") is impartial: it cannot distinguish between a living and a dead piece of theater, but only between one that makes money and one that does not. And it is these unpredictable signs of life which lead some lovers of the theater to hope that Broadway itself will change, turning at length from a show shop into a real theater.

But these hopes have been expressed regularly for thirty or forty years, and Broadway is still Broadway, much as it was in the twenties. Foreign companies come and go, but they have little visible effect on what we do, or upon the mind and taste of the daily-reviewers. New artists appear, but even the best of them seem to have less effect on the Broadway regime than it does on them. I tried to suggest how this works in my remarks on the history of our theater between the wars.

The fact is that Broadway, its structure, and its habits of mind and feeling are firmly rooted in our market-ruled society. I do not see how our "theater" can ever be more than this small and extremely precarious luxury market, unless some common vision of human nature and destiny appears among us. In the meantime the notion of theater-as-show shop expresses a deep if unadmitted feeling, on everyone's part, that our theater has as yet little of general interest or value to show.

The Mysterious Present

THE experience of the last thirty or forty years of our theater throws only a dim light on its present life. The present is notoriously hard to understand: it is a battleground of forces, some recognizable, others new. We cannot tell in advance what will survive and what will succumb.

The social and economic mechanisms which make Broadway what it is seem to be working just as before; and, as in the twenties, the new life of the theater is stirring outside the show shops. The present off-Broadway movement, like the little theaters, appears in many forms all over the country. The scene is oddly familiar, and a veteran of the twenties, pushing into a lobby on Times Square with the other paying customers, or dining by candlelight in the Village before going to see a Chekhov play in a remodeled stable, must feel that this is where he came in. But, looking more closely, one can make out differences both on and off Broadway.

Broadway has dwindled slowly over the years, as production costs have mounted there, while Hollywood, radio and TV have taken over mass entertainment. It is less popular and less sure of itself than it was thirty years ago, and it is besieged by more highbrow writers—to such a point, indeed, that Mr. Walter Kerr was impelled to explain in his recent book, *How Not to Write a Play*, that the highbrow playwrights are willfully murdering show business by trying to appeal to too intelligent an audience. The playwrights, highbrow or not, would protest, like Mr. Abe Burrows, that they are obeying the rules to the best of their ability: doing their level best to reach the largest possible audience. And I do not suppose that the older and wiser heads among Mr. Kerr's colleagues on the daily papers would care to endorse his diatribe. Very few observers would agree with him that Broadway is threatened with too much art and too many ideas. He has simply blurted out the oldest article in the show-business creed: that art or thought will frighten away the paying customers. He does, however, reflect a very general feeling that something is wrong with old-fashioned show business; and it is not inconceivable that legitimate theater, whether it call itself "Broadway" or not, may eventually revert to the eggheads by default.

As for the present off-Broadway movement, it appears that its artists are more accomplished technically, and generally more sophisticated, than their predecessors in the twenties. They know how hard it is for a beginner to crash the entertainment industry, and, on the other hand, how hard it is to have a theater outside the big market. They have a healthy respect for the money-power of the industry, but few illusions about the artistic opportunities it offers. Being young, excited about the theater, and often very talented, they attract far livelier and more discriminating audiences than those on Times Square; and they represent, as before, the new life and the new hope of the theater.

But their movement suffers, I think, from the stale but foreboding atmosphere of our postwar world, when no one, in any field, manifests a clear sense of direction. The little theaters had their mission: to introduce into this country the best of the European theaters. But the present generation has learned that lesson in college, and when they look at postwar Europe they find comparatively little that is new to encourage them, or symbolize their aspirations. The theaters of the thirties had their social motive, but now we are skeptical of all blueprints for social reform. Such considerations explain, I think, the fact that no striking new playwrights have risen to leadership off Broadway, and that the repertory to be seen in the Village now is very much like that introduced by the torch-bearers of the twenties.

Will some new sense of direction, some common if inchoate vision, be found to give the new movement form and meaning? Will some regional group, taking advantage of the confusion in New York, have the courage and insight to build a theater independently? Will a way be found to extricate the ancient art from the tyranny of the entertainment industry, so that small groups may play to small but devoted audiences? We do not know; but the new life which stubbornly sprouts, in slightly new ways year after year, seems destined to take root some day and grow at last into a mature and recognized theater.

Note on the Academic Theater

THE academic theater has for the last thirty years played an important if rather obscure part in the theatrical life of the country. It has now grown into a very large establishment, with thousands of students every year; and it produces for a large, widely scattered audience plays of every description: not only warmed-over Broadway, but classics, modern works domestic and foreign, and new works by young authors. The quality of its productions varies greatly, but it is not too much to say that, taken as a whole, the academic theater keeps the repertory alive. It also keeps many directors, designers and technical men alive: the universities are among our more useful patrons of artists, including theater artists. The academic theater thus provides a sort of subterranean continuity for our theater, cultivating its skills, remembering its resources past and present, and tiding it over the periods when the recurrent off-Broadway movements dry up. And when, as now, a new movement starts, it is fed largely from the university theaters.

Before World War I the academic theater hardly existed, and the development we have seen since then is both striking and hopeful. But even now the university theaters labor under difficulties. I do not think there is much general understanding of their potential value, either as theaters in their own right, or as part of a scheme of liberal education.

The potential value of a theater as a tool of liberal education is not hard to see in theory. Liberal educators are supposedly trying to lead the student to the sources of our tradition, and through the study of some of its masterpieces, initiate him into its basic disciplines of the mind and the spirit. But the classics (even if we could agree on what they are) are likely to seem irrelevant to our sophomores. We face in every generation the tough problem of the transmission of culture, and we find that even when the masterpieces mean something to the teacher they may say nothing to the young; we know that the arts of life and letters, when the clue is lost, may die. It is at this point that the college theater may perform a uniquely valuable service. For theatrical production seeks to restore the play to its full life, first in the performers and the imagined scene and the movement of the play as a whole, and then in the response of the audience. If the production succeeds, it means that a classic has actually been taken off the shelf, its perennial life reaffirmed.

The college theater might be thought of as analogous to a laboratory, for it demands practical, first-hand, even "creative," work on the part of both students and teachers. A college theater will seldom show the creativeness of an Olivier or a Toscanini in bringing a classic to life, but the principle is the same. Moreover, our college theaters also do contemporary works, even including some by students, teachers and other unknown playwrights, and that too has great educational value. For the receiving end of the educational process is in our own life and art, such as it is; and when a student tries something himself he can begin to see what the masters have achieved, and begin to learn to nourish and guide himself by their example.

If the educational value of the college theater is not, in fact, fully understood, that is because liberal education is itself divided and confused, and demoralized by the growth of technology and the demands of the market. Liberal educators can no longer agree on the content or methods of a curriculum—in spite of the labors of scores of "general education" committees. At the same time the need for more and more technicians of every description (engineers, chemists, accountants, statisticians) is obvious to everyone. It is much easier to provide sound technical training, which is instantly marketable, than it is to provide a liberal education; and so liberal education tends to fade out of the public consciousness altogether. Hence the despairing cries of liberal educators—not only philosophers and men of letters, but disinterested researchers in biology or physics, who also begin to fear that nothing but applied science will survive.

The college or university theater suffers from the decay of liberal education, for the theater, like the liberal arts, must assume some interest—free of the immediate struggle for power and money—in the central human situation. It also feels the pressure of the market—in its case the entertainment industry—directly. It may be asked to produce only plays that will make money, which means warmed-over Broadway. It may feel obliged to secure jobs for its graduates in TV, Hollywood, or some other part of the commercial theater. The university administration and the trustees are likely to set up a committee to watch over the university theater, consisting of three or four of their graduates who have had a play produced on Broadway, or "experience" in TV or the movies. The combined effect of such practical measures is to lose the point, and most of the potential value, of the university theater. It is no longer thought of as the protégé of liberal education, a theater reflecting the interests and tastes of the university, but as a technical school existing on the sufferance of the entertainment industry.

It is remarkable that the university theaters have been

able to maintain as much independent life as they have when their sanction has been so dubious. Their vitality is due to the fact that they do provide the theater artist's only alternative to show business. The academic theater has been the refuge, over the years, of some of our better directors, designers, teachers and playwrights; and their devoted labors account for the impressive results which the academic theater already accomplishes. But under the present dispensation it cannot go much farther. Every year the trained members of the academic theaters depart in search of the jobs which very few of them will ever get; and the small permanent staff starts once more that training which is rather disingenuously supposed to lead to Broadway or Hollywood.

What a university theater always craves if it is serious, what it would need if it were to serve liberal education and the university community fully, is a permanent theater group, a highly trained ensemble devoted not to imitating Broadway but to the classical repertory, the best modern plays, and original work in the various theater arts. I remarked that the university theater may be thought of as analogous to the laboratories of science. In the sciences pure research (though threatened) is still recognized and supported, and scientific work is organized according to an apprentice system, with the most original minds, the scouts on the frontiers of knowledge, at the top. A permanent university theater would provide such an apprentice system in the theater, offering the possibility of a career to the best artists, and giving the young and the community at large an example of what the theater can be.

Of course, for such a charming possibility to be realized, the university would have to accept the role of patron of the theater far more fully and consciously than it has yet dared to do. And one can see that, for that to happen, some common conception of the role of the university and of the role of the theater would have to make its appearance, and no one can say when, or whether, that will ever occur. In the meantime all we can do is recognize, with gratitude, the patient and immensely valuable work which the academic theater does accomplish, that of keeping the theater arts alive.

FIVE CONTEMPORARY
PLAYWRIGHTS

Three Allegorists: Brecht, Wilder, and Eliot

I

A NUMBER of contemporary playwrights, of whom Brecht, Wilder and Eliot are among the most accomplished, are now writing some form of allegory. They reject the tradition of modern realism, perhaps because little remains to be done with direct reflections of contemporary life: the pathos of the lost individual or the decaying suburb has been done to death since Chekhov. They do not seek some form of theater-poetry based on folk forms or myths or rituals, or on symbolism on the analogy of the *symboliste* poets, as so many theater artists did in the twenties. They seek to use the theater in the service of their consciously worked-out moral or philosophical ideas. They do not, however, write thesis plays à la Brieux, in which some scheme of social reform is openly debated and "proved" on the stage; nor do they write Shavian intellectual farces, in which the point is in the game of ideas itself. Their aim is not discussion in any sense, but teaching: they use the stage, the characters, and the story to demonstrate an idea which they take to be the undiscussible truth. The truths which Brecht, Wilder and Eliot propound are very different; but they all write allegory according to the literal definition in the Oxford Dictionary: "speaking otherwise than one seems to speak."

One must be very detached from the contemporary theater and its audiences in order to write allegory of this kind. Brecht, Wilder and Eliot do not expect their audiences to share their intimate perceptions, whether "realistic" or "poetic." Such detachment is the natural result of the failure of the art theaters of the twenties. After World War I much of the creative energy of the theater went into small theater groups which tried to build special audiences like those of ballet, chamber music or lyric poetry. Playwrights who worked for such groups tried to cultivate their art first and their audiences second; they were encouraged to embody their visions in the theater medium as directly as possible. In that context the thought-out indirectness of allegory seemed cumbersome and artificial. But the contemporary allegorists despair of the effort to recruit an audience of connoisseurs. They accept the commercial theater (especially Wilder and Eliot) as the only theater we can have; and the problem they set themselves is to use that non-conducting medium—necessarily *indirectly*—for their didactic purposes.

All three of these allegorists are extremely conscious of what they are doing. One can study their philosophies not only in their plays but in their theoretical writings, and all of them have written technical studies of playwriting which reveal the knowing methods they use in making their plays. But in other respects they are dissimilar and unrelated. Each of them has followed a lonely road to his achievement, and speaks through the stage as though he were alone with his undiscussible truth. For that reason it is something of a tour de force to consider them together, as though they were voices in a dialogue; as though they were devoting their thought and their art to some common enterprise in the modern theater.

Nevertheless they all seek with some success to address the mysterious modern crowd; their plays may run at the same time in the same city. And all of them are obliged to come to terms with the theater itself, stage, actors, and audience; and the art of handling those elements, though seldom studied in its full scope, is not unknown. Brecht, Wilder and Eliot seek to work out *new* theatrical forms, and Brecht owes much of his peculiar force to his direct defiance of the tradition. But one may patiently put them back into relation to the tradition by enquiring what they do with the inescapable elements of plot, characterization, language, and the conventions of make-believe. In this way one can, I think, find a basis for comparing them and for estimating the meaning of the present trend toward allegory.

II

There can be little question that Brecht in his plays teaches the Marxian dogma of the class struggle. It is evident in the plays themselves as soon as one gets the hint, and he assumes it in his theoretical writings as the one truth relevant to our times. This does not necessarily mean that he is a party member. He does not follow the tactical twistings of the party line, and he seems to have in mind an audience on this side of the Iron Curtain, one familiar with Marxism and sympathetic to it in the manner of the popular front, but not an audience of true believers. He is careful not to say anything directly which Senator McCarthy could have used to put him in jail. But in all that he writes one feels a fighting spirit as ruthless as Stalin's own, and an unwavering adherence to the small hard Marxian "truth": that nothing but the revolution has meaning or value in our lost world.

It would be a mistake to dismiss Brecht because his philosophy is brutal and myopic. For his fighting creed has served to activate one of the remarkable theatrical talents we have; and there is plenty of evidence that he

makes himself heard in our theater. The show shops
have not accepted him yet, but his reputation has been
kept alive by a few admirers, notably Mr. Eric Bentley,
who has performed a useful task in publishing and explaining him. He has been performed in academic and
off-Broadway theaters since the fellow-traveling thirties;
Roger Sessions made an opera out of his radio play, *The
Feast of Lucullus*, and as I write (1956) his *Threepenny Opera* is a fashionable and highbrow success at
the Theatre de Lys on Christopher Street in New York.
It would be important to understand his allegorical art,
and his place among those who seek to teach the theater
audience.

Brecht himself has explained his allegorical aims and
methods very clearly in numerous theoretical writings.
His basic propagandistic strategy is set forth in an essay
he wrote for underground circulation in Hitler's Germany in 1934: *Fünf Schwierigkeiten beim Schreiben
der Wahrheit* ("Five Difficulties in Writing the Truth"),
wherein the "truth" is assumed to be the sole and certain
dogma of the class struggle. His theory of playmaking,
which he calls "un-Aristotelian" or "epic," as opposed
to "dramatic," is treated in several places, and has been
well summarized by Eric Bentley in *The Playwright as
Thinker*. His strict and original use of the actor and the
stage—what might be called his theatrical style—is explained in a very interesting technical piece, "Short Description of a New Technique of the Art of Acting
Which Produces an Effect of Detachment" (*Verfrem-
dungseffekt*). These and other writings show that no one
has tried more consciously than Brecht, or with more
moral and intellectual rigor, to control the arts of the
theater for didactic purposes.

Though his aim is thus narrow and sharply defined,
he is so resourceful that his theater is marked, superfi-
cially at least, by great variety. He has known how to
nourish himself with such varied fare as the Chinese theater, Villon, Swift, modern jazz, Ben Jonson—visions of

the human comedy akin to his own. But I do not propose to try to do justice to his whole work. I wish to investigate the basis of his kind of allegory, in order to compare it with Wilder's and Eliot's.

For this purpose *Mother Courage*, to my mind one of his best plays, will serve. It is an "epic" or chronicle play of the Thirty Years' War, a string of episodes in the life of Mother Courage. She makes her precarious living by selling supplies to both armies, and tries to protect her two oafish sons, and her dumb daughter, from the perils of the war. When we last see her all three children are gone and she is destitute, but still toiling along with her empty, rickety wagon. The moral of the tale, reiterated in a different way in each scene, is that the savage situation—war as the epitome of capitalism—is intolerable, and will remain so until the revolution: "Yuh can't win."

The Prologue shows Mother Courage and her daughter Catherine riding on the wagon, which is pulled by Eilif and Swiss Cheese, the sons, to the accompaniment of a song. The first scene is then announced by a legend like a newspaper headline, which is projected on the front curtain: SPRING, 1624. IN DALARNA, SWEDEN, KING GUSTAVUS ADOLPHUS IS RECRUITING FOR THE CAMPAIGN IN POLAND. THE PROVISIONER, ANNA FIERLING, KNOWN AS CANTEEN ANNA OR MOTHER COURAGE LOSES A SON. When the curtain opens we see an Officer and a Sergeant waiting at a crossroads to snare recruits, and grumbling about their task. Mother Courage's wagon is pulled in, and a desperate and witty game begins between the soldiers, who want the boys for the Army, and Mother Courage, who tries to save them. After several unsuccessful gambits Mother Courage offers to tell their fortunes. They draw slips of paper from the Sergeant's helmet, and all get black crosses, meaning death in the war. The soldiers are impressed, and it looks for the moment as though Mother Courage has won. But the Officer offers to buy a belt, and while Mother Courage turns her back to show it to him the Sergeant sneaks off with Eilif, who is tempted by the predatory life of a soldier. Mother Courage turns around to find him gone. After a sharp exclamation of anger she orders Catherine down to take Eilif's place, and the wagon moves off. The Sergeant draws the laconic moral:

> If from the War you'd like to borrow
> Remember: the debt must be paid tomorrow!

In this scene (which has far more clarity, force and ironic pep than my summary conveys) one can see all of Brecht's principles at work. In accordance with "epic" principles of plot construction, the scene "exists for itself"; i.e., it presents a complete action. Every scene in the play is a complete playlet of this kind, and they are connected only via Mother Courage, the protagonist in each. In the Aristotelian or "dramatic" plot the play as a whole presents a complete action. Brecht regards this form as pernicious because it requires the audience to sympathize with the protagonist, and at the end a catharsis is effected and the audience is satisfied. Brecht's episodic form is supposed to insure the audience's detachment from the human content, so that their feelings will not interfere with their grasp of the Marxian moral; and at the end he does not want satisfaction but a revolutionary fighting spirit. According to his philosophy no action can be significant under capitalism: all we may do until the Revolution is comically or savagely doomed in advance to futility. Each of Mother Courage's bitter struggles demonstrates this point again.

Though each scene presents a complete action, Brecht is careful to end each one so sharply that we can feel no resolution or satisfaction at the end. Thus in this scene Mother Courage abruptly swallows the grief and anger of her defeat; she does not accept this experience or learn anything from it. She assumes that the relentless struggle will continue, and (like her author) that there is nothing to learn. Brecht hustles her offstage with her

46

wagon, beaten but tough, and we are ready for the same farcical pattern to be played through once more. This pattern has great strength and consistency, for there is no reason to suppose that the sheer animal struggle for survival—two dogs tussling for the same bone—could ever end at that level.

Brecht's handling of stage and actors—his theatrical *style*, as I have called it—is beautifully consistent with his plot and characterizations. The newspaper headline which announces the little story; the sparse stage which eliminates the "illusionism" of bourgeois realism, and the style of acting which underlies everything, are intended to assure our ironic detachment. The actors, Brecht explains (in *Short Description of a New Technique of Acting*), are not to identify themselves with the characters through sympathy, but to present the characters "with the gesture of showing." In working out this style Brecht has learned much from the Chinese theater and from neoclassic comedy, in which the actors also present the characters "with the gesture of showing." But the kind of detachment Brecht wants is very unlike the disinterested, contemplative detachment of the Chinese theater, or the smiling detachment of classic comedy. The gesture with which his actors show their characters is ironic and portentous; it detaches us from the human scene only to attach us the more firmly to the rationalized power-drive of the revolution. Thus he controls a unique and uniquely self-conscious allegorical style.

In all that Brecht has to say about the fundamental importance of acting, we feel his *theatrical* sophistication, which I suppose he acquired in the lively German theater before Hitler. Our playwrights can hardly assume any conscious art of acting, much less one flexible enough to compass a definite style. In this respect Brecht has much to teach.

Brecht, in fact, knows what he is doing as well as any playwright alive; but even so I doubt that his plays would have the desired didactic effect except upon an audience already disposed to Marxism. A properly-trained leftist audience might hiss or cheer when Mother Courage's fierce little struggles are broken off at the end of each scene, for at that point the need for revolution is "proved," and beyond the revolution lies the Marxian *Paradiso Terrestre,* where the struggle for food, shelter and sex is permanently won for all, and the human virtues which capitalism forces upon us are quite unnecessary. To reach that miraculous realm any means, however destructive, however powered with hate, might seem good. But in our bourgeois or post-bourgeois world, where the full Marxian faith cannot be assumed, Brecht's plays might have quite different effects from those he planned.

One might, for example, follow the story of Mother Courage with sympathy instead of the proper detachment, feeling the pathos of her plight even though it is not expressed. This feeling would be particularly strong at the end of the play, where her lonely courage is very touching. If one takes the play that way, one can see what Brecht calls the Aristotelian or dramatic form looming behind his Marxian tract in spite of him; for the play does present an action which ends unmistakably in Mother Courage's defeat. It would appear, then, that Brecht has not so much invented a radically new form as willfully smashed the natural one to thwart the audience's need for satisfaction, and enforce his fighting creed. Without the creed an audience would instinctively supply the "Aristotelian" pathos and resolution.

But a non-Marxian audience might, on the other hand, take the play as comic. Brecht's own inspiration, his feeling for life and its theatrical reflection, prior to his Marxism, seems to be comic rather than tragic or pathetic. His plays in performance should have speed and agility like that of comedy; and in that mood his "epic" structure—a string of lively incidents each based on the same principle—seems appropriate. Neoclassic comedy is built that way: it consists of an indefinite number of analogous incidents, each clear in advance, and laughable because the action is based upon an absurdity. Molière is the master of this form. We know, for example, that the imaginary invalid's attempts to make a career out of hypochondria, or Arnolphe's efforts to reduce love to logic, will all fail; we laugh because we see the comic protagonist not with sympathy, but as a caricature with a purely stage life, the epitome of a human attitude that we all adopt at moments. The non-Marxian, viewing Brecht's play, might be tempted to see Mother Courage with comic detachment of this kind, for her recurrent attempts to win the material fight are so clearly doomed to failure that they may be thought comic. The play would then look like a farcical aria da capo, like the endlessly repeated squabbles and intrigues which we find so entertaining in a cage of monkeys. This vision of the human plight has inspired many masters of our tradition. Dante presents it in Canto XXI and XXII of his *Hell*. One feels it in Swift, Ben Jonson, medieval farce. Because Brecht naturally shares this comic-infernal vision, he is able to use the work of some of the traditional masters to nourish his revolutionary theater. Yet, as I pointed out, Brecht does not want the kind of detachment that would make the story of Mother Courage really comic; he endeavors to do violence to that attitude, in order to prepare another act of violence, the myopic power-drive of the revolution.

Thus it seems to me that Brecht's theater, outside the context of the whole Marxian philosophy, produces puzzling and contradictory impressions. And I suppose that audiences on this side of the Iron Curtain understand him in various ways, depending on their mood and the mood of the times. In the fellow-traveling thirties the tendency was to be impressed with his firm sense of direction, so refreshing after the liberal Hamletism, and to be warmed by his sheer masculine pep, like that of Rommel, or Bulganin, or Humphrey Bogart in his gangster roles. The sleek audiences which are now enjoying his *Threepenny Opera*, with its seductively-leering tunes by Kurt Weill, its demoralized atmosphere of postwar Berlin, seem to find something quite different and hyper-sophisticated in it, a *nouveau frisson* to add to our large repertoire of pleasurable shudders.

It is evident that Brecht depends upon his fighting creed to give both form and direction to his great talent. And he has written a number of plays of great theatrical vitality, which play in the fringes of our theater and exert a wide, if subterranean, influence. But this influence appears, in our theater, to be dissociated from the Marxism Brecht wishes to teach. We respond to his savage rejection of all traditional forms and institutions, and to his triumphant reduction of the human image to that "clever and mischievous little animal" that Eliot mentions. This vision hits us all the more sharply because it is not fully accepted. It is placed in no wider context of human experience and potentiality; it has neither "comic transcendence" (Kenneth Burke's phrase) nor tragic resolution. Brecht's technical inspiration is to destroy the form of art at the very moment of exploiting it; so he leaves us unsatisfied, stimulated, needing some act of violence. But in our faithless world there is no guarantee that violence will take the Marxian-revolutionary form that Brecht wants. Violence, with us, has many illusory aims and many different faces.

III

The philosophy which Thornton Wilder presents in his plays, especially the two most famous, *Our Town* and *The Skin of Our Teeth*, is at the opposite pole from Brecht's. Brecht is exclusively concerned (like Barth in his "Theology of Crisis") with his obsessive vision of the emergency of our time. His Marxism is in essence partisan, and his theater lives by conflict. Wilder on the other hand tries to take his stance above all parties; he preaches the timeless validity of certain great old traditional ideas, and his theater is almost devoid of conflict, wooing its audience gently. Wilder's philosophy—that of a most cultivated man—is more sophisticated than Brecht's and more subtly presented. But on the evidence of the plays I think one can call it a sort of religious Platonism: deistic, but not more Christian than Unitarianism or Ethical Culture.

Brecht has paid his respects with characteristic vigor to those writers who even in our time reiterate the eternal verities: "It is true," he writes in *Fünf Schwierigkeiten*, "that Germany is falling into barbarism, and that rain falls downward. Many poets write truths of this kind. They are like painters who decorate the walls of a sinking ship with still lifes." If he read Wilder's still lifes he would characterize them in just such scornful terms. And as one turns from Brecht to Wilder one must be struck with the sudden quiet, and wonder what relevance these plays have to the actual texture of our lives. Yet Wilder's plays succeed at least as well as Brecht's in holding a modern crowd for two hours in the theater, and Wilder's art is at least as knowing, forewarned and forearmed, as Brecht's.

A very early play of Wilder's, perhaps his first, was produced by the American Laboratory Theatre in 1926, and has, I think, never been printed. It is a heavy allegory about a householder (God) who goes away on a journey, leaving his servants in charge. When he returns he finds that they have been faithful or unfaithful in various ways, and rewards them accordingly. This play is appropriately entitled *The Trumpet Shall Sound*, and it reveals Wilder's philosophy and his allegorical art at a crude, early stage. The distance between it and *Our Town* measures his extraordinary growth as technician. We have some of the experiments and finger exercises he did in the next eight years: his short plays, his adaptation of *A Doll's House*, his translation of Obey's *Viol de Lucrèce*, and his valuable technical essay, "Notes on

Playwriting." On the evidence of the plays it appears that Joyce, Gertrude Stein, Obey, and in general the literary and theatrical great of "Paris in the twenties" have been his masters. But his art has been very little studied: we marvel at his results, but have not investigated his stage magic. This essay can therefore be no more than a preliminary exploration.

Our Town is Wilder's masterpiece to date. His nostalgic evocation of Grover's Corners, New Hampshire, at the turn of the century, is fed, more than any of his other works, with the sources of poetry: old, digested memories and associations. The atmosphere of the little town convinces before all thought, as poetry does. But at the same time a New England village before World War I is a natural illustration of the faint religious humanism which Wilder wants to present allegorically. The Stage Manager-Lecturer directs our attention to the protagonist (the town) and the narrative sequence from the cradle to the grave. By the end of Act I it is evening, and we have heard *Blest Be the Tie That Binds* sung offstage by the Ladies' Choir and then whistled by Mr. Webb. George and Rebecca Gibbs, as children, are leaning out an upstairs window enjoying the moonlight:

Rebecca: I never told you about that letter that Jane Crofut got from her minister when she was sick. . . . He wrote Jane a letter and on the envelope the address was like this: It said: Jane Crofut; The Crofut Farm; Grover's Corners; Sutton County; New Hampshire; United States of America.

George: What's funny about that?

Rebecca: But listen; it's not finished: The United States of America; Continent of North America; Western Hemisphere; The Earth; The Solar System; The Universe: The Mind of God— that's what it said on the envelope.

This passage was perhaps inspired by the very similar

address which young Stephen Daedalus writes in his geography book; but it works beautifully at this point in the play, and the moral—that we live, whether we realize it or not, in the Mind of God, emerges naturally from the context of old-fashioned village childhood. In Act II Wilder uses the terrors and sentimental tears of a long-past marriage to suggest the same idea more gently; and in Act III he uses Emily's funeral and her ghostly return to earth on her fourteenth birthday for the same purpose: to present Grover's Corners *sub specie aeternitatis*. In the whole play the homesick vision and the Platonic-religious teaching work harmoniously together.

Wilder's "Notes on Playwriting" show that, like Brecht, his art of allegory is completely knowing. Like Brecht again, he stresses the conventional, make-believe quality of the stage—in opposition to the realists' "illusion"—for the purposes of allegory. All theater "lives by convention," he writes, and "a convention is an agreed-upon falsehood, a permitted lie." . . . "The convention has two functions: (1) It provokes the collaborative activity of the spectator's imagination; and (2) It raises the action from the specific to the general. . . . The stage continually strains to tell this generalized truth and it is the element of pretense that reinforces it." That is an excellent description of the way the theatrical conventions of *Our Town* work. The bare stage and the Stage Manager who directly addresses the audience or tells the actors what to do enlist the audience in make-believe: induce it to imagine the little town waking up, years ago, in the dark of early morning. At the same time the frank theatricality of these conventions warns us not to take the characters too seriously as people: they are presented only by make-believe, as half-playful illustrations of a "generalized truth." It is this "generalized truth"— that we exist in the Mind of God—which we are to watch for, and when we get it we shall have the whole point and message of the play.

Wilder maintains, in his "Notes," that all drama is essentially allegory, "A succession of events illustrating a general idea," as he puts it. "The myth, the parable, the fable are the fountainheads of all fiction," he writes, "and in them is seen most clearly the didactic, moralizing employment of a story. Modern taste shrinks from emphasizing the central idea behind the fiction, but it exists there nevertheless, supplying the unity to fantasizing, and offering a justification to what otherwise we would repudiate as mere arbitrary contrivance, pretentious lying, or individualistic emotional association-spinning." This radically Platonic view of poetry—that its only justification is that it may be a means of teaching moral truth—might be disputed at some length. But I suppose it must be the belief of all three of our contemporary allegorists; Brecht would certainly agree in principle, for his plays are very obviously constructed as "a succession of events illustrating a general idea." But it is worth noting that Brecht's "truth" is the opposite of Wilder's—which suggests that moralizing is no more immune than poetry to the human weakness for arbitrary contrivance, pretentious lying, and individualistic emotional association-spinning.

In the art of both Brecht and Wilder plotmaking is basic, for the plot, while presenting the story, must be at the same time a demonstration of the idea. Wilder relies on plotting even more than Brecht; by its means, he explains, the playwright controls stage, actors, director and designer for his purposes. "He learns to organize the play in such a way that its strength lies not in appearances beyond his control, but in the succession of events and in the unfolding of an idea, in narration." He accomplishes precisely this feat by means of the plot—the succession of events—in *Our Town*. It is primarily the narrative sequence from morning to night, from the cradle to the grave, through the marriage to the funeral, which carries the play; and it is this sequence also which continually leads to the *idea*. Brecht arranges his plots in such a way as to present onstage only struggles; he avoids all pathos on the ground that it would demoralize the audience which he is grooming for the Revolution. But Wilder, in the interest of his opposite philosophy, bases the three acts of his play precisely upon the pathos of the great commonplaces of human life, birth, marriage and death; and he shows no conflict at all.

The plot with its unfolding idea is so effective, in *Our Town*, that it almost makes the play go without reference to the individual lives of its people. But not quite: the stage is after all not the lecture platform; one must put something concrete upon it. "Because a play presupposes a crowd," Wilder writes, "the dramatist realizes that the group mind imposes upon him the necessity of treating material understandable by the greater number." It is apparently in accordance with this principle that he has selected the concrete materials of *Our Town*: the characters, which are clichés of small-town life rather than individuals; the language they speak, which (in spite of its authentic New England flavor) is distressingly close to that of plays written for high schools and Sunday schools, or to the soap operas of radio, or to vapid "family magazines." If one looks at a few passages from the play apart from the movement of the plot—George and Emily absorbing their cherry phosphates, or George having his tearful talks with his father-in-law to be—the effect is embarrassingly stale and pathetic. It is evident that Wilder himself is not much interested in George or Emily. He hardly imagines them as people, he rather invites the audience to accept them by plainly labeling them; as sentimental stereotypes of village folksiness. They are therefore understandable by the greater number, and they serve to present the story and illustrate the moral. But they betray, I think, the worst weakness of Wilder's type of allegory. The distance between the life onstage, which the audience accepts because it is so familiar in this sense, and the idea which the author has in mind is too great. The "greater number" blubbers at the platitudes of character and situation, while the author, manipulating his effects with kindly care, enjoys the improbable detachment of the Mind of God.

André Obey's *Noah* is akin to *Our Town* in several respects; I even think it possible that it may have given Wilder some of the clues for his play. *Our Town* is based on the "world" of small-town Protestantism at the turn of the century, and *Noah* upon the "world" of French peasant religion. Both plays therefore owe some of their appeal to nostalgia, and when *Noah* is played one can hardly "get" it without an effort of sympathy which may be called sentimental. But once we make-believe that vanished world, we get a vision of human life which is full of the weight of experience. The imagined characters are intensely alive; we see at every moment how Noah is groping and struggling. It is his experience which leads us to the idea—or rather the vision—which the play presents. At the end we are made to feel what Noah's faith has cost him, and therein lies the strength and the authority of the play. But the dreamy situation of *Our Town* does not cost anyone anything, and that, I think, is why the idea may strike us as sentimental and pretentious. The idea is clear; in a sense it is appropriately illustrated in the atmosphere and the customs of Grover's Corners. But it is not incarnate in the characters and the language which make up the actual texture of the play.

In spite of this weakness *Our Town* is a "natural" for Wilder and his philosophy: the basic inspiration is propitious, the remembered village and the idea to be taught do harmonize. But in *The Skin of Our Teeth* Wilder set himself an even more difficult problem: that of presenting his religious Platonism in an urban context, and at a time—the beginning of World War II—of general crisis. In that play both the theatrical virtuosity and the weakness, or limitation, of Wilder's kind of allegory are very clear.

Wilder is reported to have received the inspiration for *Skin* at a performance of *Hellza'poppin,* an extravaganza in the corniest style of old-fashioned vaudeville. But Campbell and Robinson, who attended the opening of *Skin* just after they had completed their *Skeleton Key to Finnegans Wake,* demonstrated in two well-documented articles in *The Saturday Review* that the play is a simplified dramatization of Joyce's mysterious work. There is probably no one but Wilder with enough imagination and enough understanding both of Joyce and of vaudeville to combine the two. But now that the work is done we can see what a brilliant notion it was to translate Joyce's dreamlike and ironic meditation on the eternal recurrences of human history into the ancient jokes, irrational horseplay and shameless sentimentality of burlesque. Burlesque provides Wilder with his "material understandable to the greater number," an urban folksiness corresponding to the village folksiness of *Our Town;* and *Finnegans Wake* suggests a plot-scheme and an abstract cast of characters to give narrative and rational form to the whole.

The plot of *Skin* is closely analogous to that of *Our Town.* The protagonist is Humanity, which corresponds to Grover's Corners. The three major crises on which the three acts are based, the Ice Age, the Flood, and War, correspond to Our Town's Birth, Marriage and Death. Just as Birth, Marriage and Death must be suffered by all villagers, and recur in every generation, so the crises in *Skin* are felt as common, similar, and recurrent ordeals, which must be suffered in every generation. *Skin,* like *Our Town,* is essentially a pathos, with little conflict—and that little unconvincing. The moral of the tale is the same: we have our being within the eternal verities, or the Mind of God. Thus at the end of Act I, when the Antrobus household in Excelsior, New Jersey, is getting ready to survive the Ice Age, Antrobus insists on saving Moses, Homer and the nine Muses (who are bums on the streets of New York) "to keep up our spirits." Moses and Homer each quote a bit from their works, in Hebrew and Greek respectively; and then all join in singing *Tenting Tonight*. At the end of Act II the Flood provides a more sinister hint of the truth behind our heedless lives (like the marriage in *Our Town*); and at the end of Act III bits from Spinoza, Plato, Aristotle and Genesis are quoted by members of the backstage staff. The quotations proclaim the intellectual love of God, and are supposed to be thought of as hours of the night, from nine to midnight, passing over our heads like the stars: an effect very much like the one in *Our Town*, when George and Rebecca are seen in the moonlight, with stars beyond, and beyond that the Mind of God.

All of this works very well in the theater, when "the greater number" is there to guffaw at the scenery when it leans precariously, the wise cracks aimed at the peanut gallery, and the racial jokes in the cozy style of *Abie's Irish Rose;* or to grow still and dewy-eyed when the old familiar tunes are heard. But if one happens to be feeling a little morose—smothered perhaps by so thick an atmosphere of sheer warm-heartedness—or if one tries the experiment of reading the play in cold blood, the marriage of Plato and Groucho Marx may fail to appeal. It is too evident that the "material," the actual texture, of the play, is a pastiche. The language is a collection of clichés, the characters unfused collections of familiar labels. Antrobus, for instance, consists of old jokes about the suburban householder, the middle-aged philanderer, and the Shriner on a binge, but he is also labeled the inventor of all human culture. The combination has no imaginative or intellectual unity at all. It is amusing and good-natured to set Moses, Homer and the nine Muses to singing *Tenting Tonight*, but what does Wilder's "greater number" get out of this reassuring effect? The austerity of the Ten Commandments, or tearful associations with last summer's bonfire at Camp Tamiment?

A reading of *Our Town* and *The Skin of Our Teeth* suggests that Wilder's extraordinary freedom and virtuosity in the theater is gained through eluding rather than solving the problem which most playwrights feel as basic: that of embodying form and meaning in character and language. If he had addressed himself to that problem in *Skin*, Antrobus, as the father-pilot of the race, would have had to sound a little more like Spinoza and a little less like George F. Babbitt. But Wilder has seen how it is possible to leave the "greater number" in peace with the material understandable to it, and Plato in peace in the supratemporal realm of the Mind of God. He is thus able to be "for" Plato (as politicians of every persuasion are for Peace, Freedom and Prosperity), and at the same time devote his great gifts to entertaining the crowd or "group mind."

This type of allegory is perfectly in accord with the Platonic kind of philosophy which it is designed to teach. The great Ideas are timeless, above the history of the race and the history of actual individuals. Any bit of individual or racial history will do, therefore, to "illustrate" them; but history and individual lives lack all real being: they are only shadows on the cave wall. It may be part of Wilder's consciously intended meaning that the material understandable to the greater number— comic-supplement jokes, popular tunes—*is* junky and illusory. That would be one explanation of the bodiless and powerless effect of his theater, as compared, for instance, with Brecht's. Brecht's vision is narrow and myopic, but a sense of the reality (at however brutal a level) of individual experience is truly in it. Brecht's philosophy is, of course, a philosophy of history, and leads him naturally to sharpest embodiments in the temporal struggle. But Wilder's philosophy lacks the historic dimension, and its intellectual freedom is therefore in danger of irrelevancy, pretentiousness and sentimentality.

Wilder's art, as I pointed out above, has not yet been

critically digested or expounded. Wilder occupies a unique position, between the Great Books and Parisian sophistication one way, and the entertainment industry the other way, and in our culture this region, though central, is a dark and almost uninhabited no man's land. Partly for that reason, his accomplishments must seem rather puzzling and paradoxical. The attempt which I have been making, to take him seriously as allegorizing moralist, may be much too solemn. His plays belong in the theater; they have their proper life only there, like the tricks of a stage magician. When the man pulls the rabbit out of the hat, the glamour of the occasion suffices: it is inappropriate to enquire whether he has really materialized a new creature, or only hauled out, by the ears, the same old mild vegetarian pet.

IV

Both Brecht and Wilder always and naturally write allegory: they employ the resources of poetry (when they do at all) only as means to their didactic ends. But Eliot has done more than anyone else to revivify poetry in our time and language, and his lyrics still come from the authentic source of poetry. Even as playwright he has moved slowly, and as it were reluctantly, to allegory, in response to the requirements of the theater as he felt them. From *Sweeney Agonistes* through *The Cocktail Party* he found in myths, legends and rituals, rather than in philosophic schemes alone, his clue to form and meaning; and he still tries to embody the action in language and verse. But in *The Confidential Clerk* he has, I think, written a true allegory of a type akin to Wilder's: the plot is devised and the characters selected to unfold an idea.

Eliot's philosophy is akin to Wilder's in important respects. Both are learned and cultivated men endeavoring to reaffirm what they find crucial in our tradition, instead of destroying it as Brecht does. But Eliot's philosophy is that of traditional Christianity, and he has been at pains to distinguish it from the type of abstracted, ahistoric or timeless religion-of-humanism which Wilder teaches. What Eliot wrote of the late Irving Babbitt's Humanism applies to Wilder: "alarmingly like very liberal Protestant theology of the nineteenth century: it is, in fact, a product—a by-product—of Protestant theology in its last agonies." Eliot finds so abstract and all-inclusive a philosophy too empty: if one is "for" all the good things one is in the last analysis for very little: "Boil down Horace, the Elgin Marbles, St. Francis and Goethe," he writes in criticism of Babbitt's great disciple, Norman Foerster, "and the result will be pretty thin soup." Such considerations lead him to accept a historic church and the all-important historic dimension of full Christian belief, and he is thus (unlike Wilder) in a position to feel the force of Brecht's scornful remarks about the "eternal verities." His philosophy recognizes the irreducible weight of history, and hence the significance both of the moment of time and of the individual human destiny.

It is not hard to see why Wilder, and so many other Americans of comparable intellect and culture, should embrace an abstract, timeless philosophy: there is very little else *to* embrace. Except for the Constitution we lack a common and actual "standard to which the wise and honest may repair." We learn about the varied traditions we inherit from books rather than from the actual life of our cities.

> We live in an old chaos of the sun,
> Or odd dependency of day and night,
> Or island solitude, unsponsored, free
> Of that wide water, inescapable.

Hence Babbitt's lonely Humanism, hence the hundred and one versions of the "integrated curriculum"; hence the Great Books movement, so promising in its perpetual beginnings, so sandy in its most recent *reductio ad absurdum:* Mortimer Adler's "Syntopicon." And hence, on the other hand, our pilgrimages to Europe in search of the incarnate, the still-living, tradition.

Before Wallace Stevens' beautiful "Sunday Morning," Eliot had written, in "Gerontion":

. . . Think now
History has many cunning passages, contrived corridors
And issues, deceives with whispering ambitions,
Guides us by vanities. Think now
She gives when our attention is distracted
And what she gives, gives with such supple confusions
That the giving famishes the craving. Gives too late
What's not believed in, or if still believed,
In memory only, reconsidered passion.

Such was his response to the common plight: his sense of history, and thereby of the individual's situation, responsibility, and need for a historic sense of direction, long antedates his conversion. It is necessary, I think, to remember all this in order to get some perspective on *The Confidential Clerk* and some basis for comparing it with Brecht and Wilder.

If I interpret *The Confidential Clerk* correctly, it is an allegory about Providence. All of the characters wish for things in youth which (by God's Providence) they get later in life; the moral is that we had better take care *what* we wish for, lest we get just that: we had better "make perfect our will." In the foreground are the *dramatis personae* with their more or less self-deluded wishes, in the background is the visible, historic church, which Eggerson, the first confidential clerk, has already joined, and which Colby, the second confidential clerk, seems by the end of the play to be reaching in his turn. These themes come from Eliot's lifelong preoccupation with the individual quest for spiritual fulfillment, and the cognate problems of our historic orientation. Much of his prose is devoted to exploring thorny aspects of these matters; much of his poetry, with its music and its unmistakable weight of experience, is informed by such quests. In the context of his whole work, *The Confidential Clerk* looks like a detached and comparatively serene backward glance at the course of human life—something analogous to Shakespeare's last plays, which Eliot has been echoing since "Marina." But the play as we have it has little of the concreteness of his lyric poetry. We feel in it not so much the touch of destiny itself, as an abstract theory of destiny, or Providence, which the too neat plot and the too symmetrical cast of characters are designed to demonstrate; and the whole is disguised as British parlor comedy. The result is a type of allegory oddly similar to Wilder's.

The plot of the play is based on many farcical coincidences and mistakes in identity. Sir Claude Mulhammer had two illegitimate children, Lucasta Angel and a son, whom he wished to disown, when he was young, lest they interfere with his respectable career. His wife, Lady Elizabeth, also produced a bastard in youth, whom she carelessly and timidly mislaid. As the play opens both Sir Claude and his wife are wishing for the sons they disowned so long ago. Sir Claude has engaged Colby (who he thinks is his son) as his confidential clerk, replacing Eggerson; he hopes thereby to regain him as a son; but when Lady Elizabeth sees Colby she decides he must be *her* son, since he is just the kind she would like. Colby does not wish for either parent; he wishes for a human father who (like himself) would be a mediocre but devoted musician, and (as we gradually see) a Heavenly Father, the very pattern of paternity. Lucasta pretends to be an impossible brat, reflecting Sir Claude's embarrassment at her existence; but what she really wishes for is a respectable marriage. Her suitor, B. Kaghan, wishes for the same, though he defensively stresses his own vulgarity. In the pat *dénouement* it appears that B. Kaghan is really Lady Elizabeth's son; he marries Lucasta and so they both get their modest but not-wrong wishes for social position and respectable marriage. Colby turns out to be the son of a second-rate church organist, and when we last see him he is planning to be the organist in Eggerson's suburban church and eventually take orders. Colby thus takes first prize in the Providential distribution of awards: he will become God's confidential clerk, instead of Sir Claude's. As for Sir Claude and Lady Elizabeth, Providence rewards them according to their deluded youthful wishes: Lady Elizabeth gets the kind of son she deserves, not the kind she wishes for, and Sir Claude gets no son at all.

This story, which covers the vicissitudes of several generations—voyages, separations, losings and findings—reminds one of the complicated tales which the Renaissance inherited from Hellenistic times, often via Roman comedy. Shakespeare used such a story for farcical purposes in *The Comedy of Errors*, and for purposes analogous to that of our interminable soap operas, in *Pericles, Prince of Tyre, A Winter's Tale*, and *Cymbeline*. Eliot uses both aspects of his plot: to provide a string of farcical situations in Sir Claude's household, and also (as the past is gradually revealed) illustrations of the relation between human wishes and God's Providence. This scheme is very promising for Eliot's allegorical purposes; and it fits our time of dim displaced persons as well as it did late antiquity, another time of exiles groping in the confusion of several demoralized cultural traditions. But just because this scheme is so suggestive and ideally demands so much, Eliot is much less successful in presenting it in the theater than Wilder is with his more consistently abstract ideas.

Like Wilder Eliot relies primarily on the plot to demonstrate his idea; and the plot does demonstrate it with absurd neatness. But Wilder's plots are based on a generalized protagonist (Our Town, or Humanity), and on general situations like death or war, all of which harmonizes with his general or "timeless" philosophy. In Wilder's theater the weak and trite individual characters matter comparatively little; but Eliot's philosophy focuses upon individual destiny in history, and for that reason the artificiality of the plot and the perfunctory nature of the characters are all but fatal. Eliot's scheme makes the classic demand of drama: that the action be embodied in imagined individual lives, while it is just this requirement that Wilder so dexterously by-passes.

In *The Confidential Clerk* Colby occupies the position of the "central awareness," as James called it, and it is therefore that character who shows most clearly where the trouble lies. Lady Elizabeth, Eggerson, perhaps even Lucasta, are objectified enough: they are actable, and adequate for their minor roles in the play. But Colby, as he moves from his early bewilderment, when he hardly knows what he "wishes for," to the end, when his direction is clear, should lead the audience, through understanding and sympathy with his experience, to get the form, the meaning and the validity of the whole action. But Colby is "there" only as an all-too-clear unrealized intention, plus the clothes and manners of any well-brought-up young man. We cannot take his inner being or his experiences seriously, and so we get them at the conceptual level only. His route to God *may* be there, but since we neither feel nor imagine it, we are inclined to shrug it off as no more than one more theoretical possibility.

In saying that drama classically demands that the action be "incarnate" in individual lives I am not thinking of the demands of photographic realism. Eliot and Wilder both provide photographs. What I am thinking of is the kind of imaginative and actable consistency we feel in "Gerontion," or "Journey of the Magi," or "Song for Simeon." The *personae* whose voices we hear in those lyrics are living in the sense I mean. In his lyrics Eliot is a master of this kind of individuation, but when he writes for the theater he has great difficulty in objectifying the life of his protagonist. In *Murder in the Cathedral*, Thomas à Becket, after explaining himself at great length, must still complain, "How should you know what I do?" By the time we reach Colby we have a figure which exists, along with the furniture, in Sir Claude's study, but not in that realm of the spirit where his author feels the essence of the human drama to be. This sad result must be at least partly blamed on the theater for which Eliot writes.

In the fragmentary *Sweeney Agonistes* Eliot was working in a music-hall medium, probably under the influence of Cocteau; in *Murder in the Cathedral* he was writing for a church. But since then he has been writing for the professional London theater: the "group mind" of the carriage trade, as distinguished from Wilder's much folksier crowd. And the closer he gets to "the land of lobelias and tennis flannels," as he called it in *The Rock:* "decent godless people:/Their only monument the asphalt road/And a thousand lost golf balls," the farther he is from his own inspiration. The whole medium or "material" of polite comedy, the sleek, photographic interiors, the conventional cast of characters, the narrow but unavoidable requirements of the comic intrigue, leaves him little room for theatrical invention, little chance to make the stage itself express his meaning or feeling. In this respect the art of *The Confidential Clerk* is meager indeed, when compared with the theatrical virtuosity of Wilder's plays. The course of Eliot's prolonged assault on the professional British theater is discouragingly close to Henry James's experience when he tried, more than two generations ago, to launch his dramatic vision in the London theater, and concluded that he had been obliged to "throw the cargo overboard to save the ship."

The New York production of *The Confidential Clerk* looked like an unusually well-written British comedy, with an undertone of serious meaning which neither the actors nor the audience knew quite what to do with. The excellent cast disregarded the versification and played up the farcical situations which it felt the audience might enjoy. But if one reads the play, listening for the four stresses per line, taking the language as music rather than the dialogue of characters in particular situations, one may from time to time catch a faint melody which, I think, suggests Eliot's real inspiration. In the final scene Mrs. Guzzard, the woman who took charge of the mislaid bastards years ago, a kind of *dea ex machina*, points the moral which the plot has demonstrated:

Thén I will say good-býe. You have áll had your wísh
In one fórm or anóther. You and Í, Sir Cláude,
Had óur wishes twénty-five yéars agó:
But we fáiled to obsérve, when we hád our wíshes,
That thére was a tíme-limit cláuse in the cóntract.

Somewhere far behind the visible and audible comedy is a resigned and lyric meditation on the ways of Providence. It is of that, I think, that Eliot wishes to speak; but the distance between that meaning and what his comedy *seems* to say is too great: the two together do not make a theatrically viable form of allegory.

V

It is the peculiarity of the kind of allegory represented by Brecht, Wilder and Eliot that the author *assumes* the truth and the acceptability of the moral to be taught. It is this which distinguishes contemporary allegory from the old-fashioned thesis-play, in which the thesis is directly discussed and supposedly proved to the satisfaction of all parties to the dispute. Thus Brecht assumes his Marxian doctrine as something his audience can get through apothegmatic references, signals instantly clear to those who know. And in analogous ways Wilder and Eliot assume their Platonic or religious philosophies, reminding their audiences of the ancient truths rather than arguing, or trying to induce a fresh perception. All three allegorists, in other words, write "as if" their audiences were with them: this attitude is the basis of their didactic strategies.

But in order to teach that way in the theater, each playwright must put on the stage some aspect of human life, some mode of action, which his audience will recognize, and which at the same time harmonizes with the idea to be taught. All of them would presumably accept Wilder's dictum, that the basis of the playwright's art is in "the unfolding of an idea"; yet each one, in the necessary effort to bring life to the stage, instinctively "imitates an action." In each case the *action* of the play is the connecting link between the audience and the author's ideas. And I believe that the action is a better index of the *actual* spiritual content of the plays than the ideas which the playwrights wish to teach.

Thus Wilder writes "as if" we were all good-hearted home folks together (his diagnosis of the assumption underlying our popular entertainment): "I don't think the theater is a place where people's feelings ought to be hurt," says Sabina in *The Skin of Our Teeth*. And in *Our Town* we read, in the "serious talk" that George and Emily have in their late teens:

Emily: I always expect a man to be perfect and I think he should be.

George: Oh . . . I don't think it's possible to be perfect, Emily.

Emily: Well, my father is, and as far as I can see your father is. There's no reason on earth why you shouldn't be too.

George: Well, Emily . . . I feel it's the other way round. That men aren't naturally good; but girls are. Like you and your mother and my mother.

George and Emily, like Sabina and the other characters in Wilder's two plays, are trying to "feel good," and it is that action which the audience sympathetically imitates, sharing its Sunday school righteousness and its smiling tears of delicious embarrassment. Wilder counts on the analogy between this bathetic attempt to feel good and the action recommended in the classic counsel: "Be ye therefore perfect even as your Father in heaven is perfect." Through this analogy he proposes to remind us of the Good, the True and the Beautiful in the Mind of God. But the analogy, if it exists, is extremely remote; and the idea, if one tries to apprehend it at any sort of adult level, is not incarnate in the action. It remains a bodiless allusion, hardly appropriate to the squirms and sniffles we indulge in while feeling good with George and Emily.

Brecht, approaching the modern crowd from an opposite angle, writes "as if" we were all condemned to the single-minded pursuit of material satisfaction, nimbly filching each other's shirts (and wives) in the myopic old game of pleasure and power. The idea he wishes to teach—by allusion—is the Marxian Utopian idealism; but what gives his plays their carrying power is again the least common denominator of action. It is the sardonic hilarity of the squabble that we share and enjoy.

Eliot is of course a far more serious and searching moralist than Wilder or Brecht. And the plan of *The Confidential Clerk* calls for a more balanced, varied and comprehensive composition of analogous actions leading to the perception of an order, rather than to a mere idea. The action, according to plan, would be "to discover what I really wish for." At the bottom of the scale would be Sir Claude, with his timid, snobbish diagnosis of his wishes; at the top, Colby, when he finally sees that his true wish would be obedience to God. But in order to establish contact with the audience he has in mind Eliot is obliged to write "as if" we were all brought up in good society, careful in matters of taste, keeping a stiff upper lip for politeness' sake; embarrassed by metaphysics. And on this basis, he, like Wilder, can realize only a very reduced version of the action his plot calls for. What we actually see and feel in that drawing room are plausible types endeavoring to formulate their dim wishes within the limits of social convention. And in the ensuing conversations there is little to choose between Colby and Sir Claude: the action, thus circumscribed, is so narrow that the difference between salvation and damnation is hardly perceptible. The hierarchy Eliot wishes to teach is present only as it is somewhat artificially alluded to in talk.

Wilder and Eliot both seek to teach certain ideas derived from the central religious-humanistic tradition, and in thinking over their results one is led to wonder—rather idly, perhaps—what it would take to reincarnate the ancient vision. Eliot speaks, in his essay on Baudelaire, of "the adjustment of the natural to the spiritual, of the bestial to the human, and the human to the supernatural." One can see how this formula might apply to *Lear*, for example: the natural, the spiritual, the bestial, the human and the supernatural are all present with the weight and authority of experience; all alive with the imagined lives of the characters and their relationships; all "adjusted" to one another in countless suggestive ways. But one cannot see how, even if a genius like Shakespeare were available, any such comprehensive picture of human nature and destiny could be squeezed into our show shops. Eliot and Wilder do not, of course, make the attempt. Their plays are designed in accordance with their diagnoses of the "group mind" of the contemporary theater. Therein is their originality, and also their technical interest and their significance as signs of the times. It is discouraging to find that they connect with their audiences only by way of nostalgia, flattering daydream, or "wish"—finding thereby no way to incarnate their meanings, teaching only by concepts and allusion.

Brecht's plays do not have this bodiless quality. His materialistic philosophy does not connote the problem of "incarnation": you might say that his characters are *all* "carne," and that the destructive half of his revolu-

tionary creed—each thing meeting in mere oppugnancy—
is brilliantly realized in his theater. But the other half,
the Marxian Utopia, is at least as unrealized as Eliot's
and Wilder's moral and religious ideas. If one regards
Brecht as a Marxian idealist one may feel in his work as
well as in that of Wilder and Eliot, the force of Yeats's
nightmare:

> Things fall apart; the centre cannot hold;
> Mere anarchy is loosed upon the world,
> The blood-dimmed tide is loosed, and everywhere
> The ceremony of innocence is drowned;
> The best lack all conviction, while the worst
> Are full of passionate intensity.

The aims of those who seek to make an allegorical
form for the modern theater, in order to teach the group
mind indirectly, by way of some mode of action which
they can recognize and accept, would seem to be natural
and right. But it is hard to see how this effort can get
much farther in our theater as it is. Brecht, Wilder and
Eliot, with their varied talents and their extraordinary
technical resourcefulness, have shown us what is possible in that line.

Joyce's *Exiles*

Exiles was written during the spring of 1914, the year in which *Dubliners* was published, *Portrait of the Artist as a Young Man* completed, and *Ulysses* begun. It is a play of the end of youth, or the knowing threshold of maturity,

> En l'an trentiesme de mon aage
> Que toutes mes hontes j'ay beues.

Joyce was in complete possession of himself and his literary powers. He paused for a last look at the soul which Stephen Daedalus had been impiously constructing, a vehicle winged for the exploration of new and perhaps forbidden realms, a fresh "conscience of his race." The *Portrait* shows us the process of construction; *Exiles* gives us the completed masterpiece. The timeless artifact of Richard Rowan is an image on the mind's eye "luminously apprehended as self-bounded and self-contained," a work of art as Stephen Daedalus defines art. *Exiles* is thus at once, and by the same token, a singularly elegant and self-conscious piece of dramaturgy, and a brilliant image of the ethical being of the young Joyce. When the author finished it and returned to his labors on *Ulysses* he lost interest for good in the "artist as man," and his vitality passed into the narrative

72

itself and its characters. Joyce himself is henceforth lost to sight behind or beyond his work.

Exiles is thus important for the understanding both of Joyce and of modern drama between *Peer Gynt,* say, and *Murder in the Cathedral;* but it has been studied less than any of the other works in the canon. The more obvious wealth and virtuosity of *Ulysses* and the more explicit discursive clarity of *Portrait of the Artist* have eclipsed it. It is in itself an austere and difficult work. Being naturalistic drama, it represents in its three acts as much life and thought as we are accustomed to getting in the looser bulk of a long novel. The reader must let his thought and imagination play over the characters and their stories a long time if he is to appreciate the weight of experience which they can convey. He must recall what he knows about Joyce, Dublin, Ibsen, and the Scholastic philosophy which is Rowan-Joyce's favorite weapon. To enjoy the play's beauty of form, one must think of Ibsen's dramaturgy, which was Joyce's starting point, as well as of Stephen Daedalus's doctrines of art. The present essay is intended to provide a sample of such an analysis, with some of the facts and ideas which a reader would need really to enjoy the play.

The Spirit of Ibsen

Mr. Herbert Gorman says in his excellent biography* that in *Exiles* Joyce was paying his final compliment to the influence of Ibsen. This influence—"the spirit of Ibsen, like a keen wind, a spirit of wayward boyish beauty"—Joyce felt at the beginning of his career and never disowned. Even as late as 1934, when he saw a production of *Ghosts* in Paris, he could write a poem in

* *James Joyce,* by Herbert Gorman, Farrar and Rinehart, 1939. Many of the facts in this essay are taken from Mr. Gorman's study, which contains many writings by Joyce which have not been published elsewhere.

which he playfully pictured himself as "the ghost of Captain Alving," a "Viking" whose ship was scuttled. Whenever Joyce turned his attention to the figure he cut as a man, he got the picture of one of Ibsen's dispossessed but unregenerate Vikings, before life, exiled or ghostly.

When We Dead Awaken was the play of Ibsen's which possessed Joyce's imagination above all the others. It was the subject of his first literary effort, when he was about eighteen, an article in the *Fortnightly Review,* after which he wrote Ibsen a proud and touching letter, saluting him as guide, master and friend. *Exiles* was written thirteen years after the article; but it is parallel in so many ways to *When We Dead Awaken* that it may be read as a further commentary upon it. Both plays are about the tragic contradiction between love and complete spiritual freedom and integrity: Rowan-Joyce's explanation to Bertha, "to hold you by no bonds, even of love, to be united with you in body and soul in utter nakedness—for this I longed," directly echoes the affair between Rubek-Ibsen and his Irene, which was also to have been a relationship of "frank, utter nakedness." The casts of characters in the two plays are similar: two men and two women, tied together yet kept apart by their various versions of love and freedom, and isolated, as a group, by the dreary anarchy, the moral emptiness, of the modern world. In both the central character is a portrait of the artist, Rubek the sculptor corresponding to Rowan the writer. But Rubek is at the latter end of life, while Rowan is at the beginning; and though Joyce has taken an Ibsenesque theme, he has played another and perhaps final variation upon it. Richard Rowan is forewarned and forearmed by Ibsen's terrible example, and he is (as he put it in a defiant poem addressed to his Dublin colleagues) "steeled" as Ibsen was not "in the school of old Aquinas." Exile, defiantly and adventurously accepted, replaces the literal death which Ibsen, exhausted, near hysteria, felt to be so near.

When We Dead Awaken is so profoundly gloomy that

one might not see, at first, why it should have inspired a very young man, even Joyce, with the lust for life and high endeavor. Professor Rubek, the sculptor, who had started out in youth with Irene "to the world's end and to the end of life," to serve life and love and art "in frank, utter nakedness," now finds himself in the triviality of a summer resort, not at the end but at the vulgarization of that life, love and art which he still rather frantically craves. His present wife, Maia, is seduced by a hard-drinking wolf- and woman-hunter; and when Irene reappears he can only resolve his "posthumous" affair with her by a suicidal expedition to the top of the mountain in a storm,

> Surexcité par Emporheben
> Au grand air de Bergsteigleben.

It is Ibsen's vision of the end of his road—one of the many pictures of the disillusioned fag end of romanticism, like D. H. Lawrence's captain in *The Captain's Doll*, absurdly sliding about on the glacier to the amusement of the tourists, or Eliot's violated young girl in the beginning of *The Waste Land*, who feels free in the mountains and goes south in the winter. In this play moreover, Ibsen's discouragement seems to be connected with a weakening of his powers as a dramatist. The characters are a little thin and diagrammatic, by his standard; the symbolism a little crude and ill-digested. If you project this enfeeblement a little farther you reach the nerve-wracking helplessness of O'Neill. And yet, *When We Dead Awaken* still has that quality which distinguished Ibsen, and Joyce after him: "The lamp of the spirit" still burns, as Henry James put it, "as in tasteless parlors, with the flame practically exposed." It is Ibsen's relentless clarity of vision, the moral courage to accept all consequences, that inspired the young Joyce. It must have seemed to him to promise life itself, compared either with the unproductive traditionalism of the Church, as he saw it, or with the evasive mists of the

Irish Renaissance. He accepted the perils of this individual integrity of vision, made this conception of the heroic modern artist his own, completing it and bringing it to rest in the soberer light of "old Aquinas."

When We Dead Awaken may be described as a quest, by Rubek and the others, for an object ("Life" or "Freedom") which is symbolized by the lonely snow peaks. But Richard Rowan, as we see him in *Exiles*, is no longer seeking, changing or developing. He recognizes the half-understood "language of his youth"—Wagnerian, or Nietzschean, or Ibsenesque—when Robert Hand reminds him of it; but he now disowns it. He places it, along with its confused motivations (to which Beatrice and Robert and even Bertha are still subject) in the light of his present motionless clarity. When Richard is on the scene he demonstrates the romantic motives of his former friends, in their cowardice or dishonesty, like a priest or a physician, and by a process of question and answer which reminds one of the *Quaestiones* of the *Summa*. And because of Richard's almost hypnotic influence, the result of his superior courage and intelligence, the other characters are always explaining themselves to each other even when Richard is not physically present.

Because Joyce is so richly aware of the "cultural conditioning" of his Dublin friends—those nets of loyalty, habit, modes of thought and feeling put out to catch the soul, but which he has carefully eluded—his demonstrations of Beatrice Justice and of Robert Hand are demonstrations of the *Zeitgeist* also in many of its components. Under Richard's sad and unmalicious questioning, Beatrice is revealed as Protestant, musical and celibate. It is the pride and scorn in her heart which attached her, in youth, to Richard; her cowardice, her inability to give herself freely, which now eternally separates her from him, in fact and in essence. Behind her we see many a provincial Protestant community, with its undernourished rebels. She is like an Ibsen character caught, so to speak, in the act—brought guiltily and hopelessly to rest in the light of Richard's understanding.

Robert Hand, as we discover in the great scene in the second act between him and Richard, has been seduced by another and apparently opposite face of the Demon of the Absolute. He too can claim kinship with Richard on the basis of the impulses and slogans of their youth:

Robert: All life is a conquest, the victory of human passion over the commandments of cowardice. . . . The blinding instant of passion alone—passion, free, unashamed, irresistible—that is the only gate by which we can escape from the misery of what slaves call life. Is not this the language of your own youth that I heard so often from you in this very place where we are sitting now? Have you changed?

Richard: (*Passes his hand across his brow.*) Yes. It is the language of my youth.

It is the language of their youth, and it sounds like the Nietzsche of *The Birth of Tragedy,* or the Wagner of *Tristan.* But Richard is now as completely separated from Robert, in fact and in essence, as he is from Beatrice. The place where they are now sitting has been transformed by Robert's *fin de siècle* taste: the lamps are pink-shaded, the air perfumed, Robert wears an arty velvet jacket. The soft sounds of *Tannhäuser,* which Robert plays on the piano at the opening of the scene, have replaced the desperation of the *Liebestod.* And under Richard's grave questioning we see that Robert's attempt to seduce Bertha has none of the heroic intransigence of the demand for Love or Death, or for the two as one. It is not even certain that he wants Bertha specifically; perhaps it is rather, through her, the destruction or possession of Richard. He seeks, as Richard brings out, to "know in soul and body, in a hundred forms, and ever restlessly, what some old theologian, Duns Scotus, I think, called a death of the spirit." His

77

erotic "giving" appears to be, as much as Beatrice's timid spiritual parsimony, an evasion of that complete, individual ethical awareness which Richard represents.

It is characteristic of Joyce that he should present Robert not only with sadness but with ironical humor. When Robert packs his bag (as we learn in the third act) Bertha is afraid he is going to commit suicide. Apparently she has taken his Wagnerian blarney at face value. But he is only going to visit his respectable cousin in England, seeking relief (or spiritual death) in a gentler form. Robert Hand is one of Joyce's careful portraits of the warm-hearted Irishman of irresistible charm.

All of the characters in *Exiles* were tempted in youth by heroic postures, but at the time which the play shows, only Richard's heroism is unbroken, only his intellectual integrity intact. This enables him, not to condemn, but to perceive, everyone. If there is a moral to the play, it is against his principles to give or even suggest it. Yet Rowan-Joyce's undimmed awareness is the center of the composition at every level, the clue at once to its matter and its form. To understand this, and to appreciate the play's perfection of form, one must reflect on Stephen Daedalus's doctrines of art.

The Artist as Hero

The Modern Library editions of Joyce's works carry the familiar device of a sprightly naked figure prancing, presumably to the relief of ignorant humanity, with a streaming torch. The effect is to associate Joyce's work with the Promethean themes of "modern" literature. Stephen-Richard-Joyce would reject the kinship with other modern writers which this implies. When he toys with the notion of a mythic parallel to his destiny he chooses not Prometheus but Daedalus. The artist in his flight is as impatient as Prometheus of divine restraints, but he is not, like Prometheus, attached to the service of humanity. He ascends for the exhilaration of the ride, and to satisfy his own nature. The art whereby he rises is almost identical with the flight, as the flight is with his being. His being and his art are both self-contained, and both "free" alike of God and of man.

The originality of this conception of art and individuality may be grasped by comparing Richard Rowan, the center of *Exiles*, with Rubek, the center of *When We Dead Awaken*. Rubek feels indissoluble analogies between his drive for the peaks, the yearnings of the other characters, and the *Zeitgeist*, to which he appeals in the audience. He is (for all his clarity) partly moved by passion, exploring a mystery he still feels as both common and ultimate. The motivation of the play as a whole (its forward movement in time) is thus, as Aristotle would put it, both ethical and pathetic. Hence there is a Bacchic, or choral, or mob element—call it what you will—in Ibsen's play; as though Ibsen still felt that some god or demon *might* be speaking, somehow, in the voice of individual passion or in the solicitations of common feeling. It is this "pathetic motivation" which Joyce was at great pains to eliminate from the character of Richard, and also from his play, as the clue to its temporal progression or its composition. It is not that Richard is unfeeling, but that he rejects, completely, his feelings and others' as a guide to action. "God," says Stephen Daedalus, "is a cry in the street." And it is not that he does not intend his play to move us, but rather that esthetic pleasure is to follow perception of the object he is constructing. Accordingly, in the development of the composition, it is the eye of the mind which moves, movingly, heroically, "free" of feeling.

Richard Rowan's complete rejection of "the mob in himself," as Mr. T. S. Eliot has put it, makes his agony very much like that of the "purely heroic" drama of French seventeenth-century rationalism. Undeluded, unsurprisable, fixed on the tragic split between freedom and intellectual integrity on one side and love on the other, he is now brother to the heroes of Racine and Corneille who face without flinching the irreconcilable conflict of Reason and Duty against Love or Passion. He is as profoundly irreligious as they, with their Kantian autonomy of intellect, whose being consists in decreeing the laws of its own nature. Like them, he is so complete a hero that he can never become a scapegoat, never suffer a change of heart or a new insight, to the regeneration of his own or the public life. The tragic flaw is not in him, but in his metaphysical situation, which he demonstrates, beneath the changing facts and feelings of concrete experience, as ever the same. At Richard's fixed and ultimate point, the esthetic image is as ever present in the mind's eye as the moral object is. Hence his drama is basically a demonstration, esthetic, rational —like that of Racine. It is neoclassic rather than classic; for it carefully eschews the *ritual* sacrifice which is the basis of Sophoclean drama, and which Ibsen rediscovers, in a way, and in his naturalistic terms.*

A careful reading of *Exiles* will show how self-consciously Richard rejects any sacrificial motive, either in himself or in others. "There is a faith still stranger," he coldly remarks to Robert, "than the faith of a disciple in his master: the faith of the master in the disciple who will betray him." Robert and Beatrice have both presented themselves as his rather treacherous disciples, ostensibly offering the sacrifice of their faith and service, actually wishing also to join him by bringing him down to their level or destroying his integrity. Richard sees himself as potentially a martyr or type of Christ, but (whether he feels that he knows too much, or is committed to another destiny) he refuses the role and all its relationships as both shameful and dishonest. He will neither take the responsibility of being anyone's "master" nor allow anyone else to sacrifice anything to a supposed loyalty to him. This amounts, in his strict interpretation, to utter solitude.

* Mr. Kenneth Burke has remarked that "ritual drama" moves in a rhythm of "purpose to passion to perception." *Exiles* is fixed at "perception."

One may notice parenthetically how similar Richard's plight is to that of Eliot's Thomas of Canterbury. Thomas aspires to sainthood, the Sophoclean or Christian role of scapegoat, which Richard won't have; but he discovers that a self-appointed scapegoat is as irrelevant as a self-appointed hero. It is, I think, a question, whether even his martyrdom, as Eliot shows it, really saves him from the machinery of his own intellect and from "damnation in pride."

It is comparatively easy for Richard to separate himself from Robert and Beatrice, but Bertha, by whom he has a child, with whom he is trying to live in "frank, utter nakedness" of soul, is a hostage to the others and to the disorderly world of concrete experience. It is in his relation to Bertha that the split between his intellectual integrity and love—never, in any of its forms, quite digestible by the intellect; always, in our experience, somewhat ambiguous—becomes truly tragic. The scenes between Richard and Bertha, especially the last one, are as beautiful as any love scenes in modern drama. In their quietness, their tender refusal of a passion which is always present, they are like the grave farewells of Racine's monarchs, who are poised for five acts on that point of vibrant stillness, that motionless turn from love to duty. Yet they differ from Racine's scenes in one important respect: Richard is the only character on or off stage who understands the issues, while in Racine or Corneille the characters and the audience are all supposed to share the common light and glory of Reason, which is also duty, the basis of manners, the social order, and the state. The neoclassic hero's integrity is identical with his place, his responsibility, and his *gloire;* but Richard's is presented as the law of his own nature only, and hence as his exile and his invisibility. Titus's freedom from the servitude to passion is the same as Bérénice's, but the freedom which Richard has attaches and subjects Bertha, because she cannot understand it. The "reasons of his heart" she grasps, but the reasons of his reason, which he always obeys, she does not see; and between his intellectual integrity and her love she is held prisoner more completely than she could have been by the ritual sacrifice of the conventional marriage promise.

Stephen Daedalus's theories of art, as he explains them to the unwilling Lynch, throw a good deal of light upon the connections between Joyce's static, neoclassic conception of drama and his absolute ethical individualism. "The tragic emotion is static. Or rather the dramatic emotion is. The feelings excited by improper art are kinetic, desire or loathing. . . . The arts which excite them, pornographical or didactic, are therefore improper arts." He interprets this with the utmost strictness, for he maintains later that art, as such, has no meanings whatever outside itself. He is discussing Aquinas on beauty. He accepts *integritas* and *consonantia,* but he mistrusts *claritas* as perhaps imperiling the independence of art. "I thought he might mean that *claritas* was the artistic discovery and representation of the divine purpose in anything, or a force of generalization which would make the esthetic image a universal one, make it outshine its proper conditions. But that is literary talk. I understand it so. When you have apprehended that basket as one thing and have then analysed it according to its form and apprehended it as a thing you make the only synthesis which is logically and esthetically permissible. You see that it is that thing which it is and no other thing. The radiance of which he speaks is the scholastic *quidditas,* the whatness of a thing. This supreme quality is felt by the artist when the esthetic image is first conceived in his imagination."

One is reminded of Richard's esthetic and logical gratification when he exclaims to Bertha, "I see you as you are"; of his pitying perception, after questioning, of Beatrice "as she is" in her timid pride and scorn; of his unavailing insistence that the others see him "as he is." Stephen-Richard takes the quiddity of the work of art or of the person as absolute and unrelated. The dramatic form, Stephen explains, is "the form wherein the artist presents his image in immediate relation to others," and later, "the dramatic form is reached when the vitality which has flowed and eddied around each person fills every person with such vital force that he or she assumes a proper and intangible esthetic life." In *Exiles* each person has indeed an intangible esthetic life which is itself and no other thing so completely that it appears to us like one of the images in Dante's Hell: cut off, final, unchanging, and brilliant in its irrelevancy, against the surrounding darkness.

It is clear that Stephen-Richard-Joyce took from Aquinas and Aristotle chiefly a rigorous intellectual method with which to "rationalize" his own individualism and the absolute art he sought. Aquinas with his realism has no doubt of the quiddity, the integral actuality of things, persons and works of art. But he sees them in a vast web of analogical relationships ultimately sustained and clarified in God. The individual has his inner harmony and intelligibility, yet is intelligible ultimately only by analogy with other things. Aristotle's theory of drama is in effect similar: action, which all the characters share by analogy, and not character, he took to be its fundamental matter, the object which it imitates. Here too the individual, though actual at any moment, is not absolute in a Joycean way, or static like the heroes of rationalism.

The divergence from Aquinas and Aristotle is completely self-conscious and consistent. Joyce must diverge at this point, making his Thomism godless, interpreting Aristotle in a neoclassic sense, if the freedom of exile is to have its demonic completeness. One may well ask, I think, whether the drama to end all dramas, which results, is performable. Certainly it is actable "in itself," for though Joyce has nothing to say about action, he apprehends directly the psychic movements of every character at every moment, and thus composes always, like Ibsen, in "the form of action," the direct histrionic medium. The play has its paradoxical unity of action: the demonstration by all the characters in their various ways of their eternally separate "quiddities." It would be difficult to act properly, for the part of Richard would make terrible demands on the insight of any actor, and the play as a whole requires the same patient attention to naturalistic detail as Ibsen does. But the real question of its performability is of another order: the play as a whole has the same anomalous relation to its hypothetical audience as Richard has to the other characters.

We are warned in a thousand ways to perceive Richard and his drama as simply unique. Yet there is Stephen's definition of Pity and Terror. "Pity is the feeling which arrests the mind in the presence of whatsoever is grave and constant in human sufferings and unites it with the human sufferer. Terror is the feeling which arrests the mind in the presence of whatsoever is grave and constant in human suffering and unites it with the secret cause." In this doctrine the esthetic pleasure in the perception of images of human life would seem to depend, precisely, upon "some force of generalization." If so, Joyce intended his audience, once the uniqueness of the esthetic object had been perceived, to make it intelligible and acceptable by analogies, as the present essay has tried to do. Richard is both like the unique birdman, moved by a "spirit of wayward, boyish beauty," to an impossible stunt, and the pagan sages whom Dante meets in Hell between the nameless hordes of the trimmers and Paolo and Francesca with their windy wailing. Their intellect, which does not know God, raises a hemisphere of light in the darkness, and quiets the air, in which they live "in desire but without hope." Both are images of exile and solitude, which is grave and constant enough in human experience, full enough of pity and terror to satisfy an audience which came to understand it.

Don Perlimplín: Lorca's Theater-Poetry

FOR something like forty years poets in English-speaking countries have been trying to write poetic drama for the modern stage. This movement, if something so scattered and diverse may be called a movement, stems largely from Yeats and Eliot. Their plays are still the best modern poetic drama we have, and their theories still define the prevailing conception of poetic drama. But no one is quite satisfied with the results. We still lack a poetic theater-form comparable to those of more fortunate ages, or to the "unpoetic" convention of modern realism. Poetic drama in English remains unsure of itself, highbrow and cultish—unless *Elizabeth the Queen, Venus Observed,* and *The Cocktail Party,* which are fairly well accepted in the show shops, are to be called poetic drama.

Federico García Lorca also wrote poetic drama, very much as Yeats and Eliot have taught us to understand it, yet his plays are neither cultish nor middle-brow-Ersatz: they are theater-poetry which lives naturally on the modern stage. Lorca did very little theorizing, but he found, at a very early age, in pre-Franco Spain, singularly direct ways to use the stage for the purposes of poetry. It is true that he is not a creature of the commercial theater. Madrid in his time had a theater corresponding to Broadway, but Lorca was always in more or less hidden opposition to it. He was the director of "La Barraca," a group of University players which was subsidized by the government and toured the provincial towns and cities of Spain with a repertory of classics. It is evident that his own plays owe a great deal to this experience. La Barraca found an "off-Broadway" audience in Spain, and since then Lorca's plays have found audiences in France, Switzerland, Germany, Mexico, South America, and college towns all over this country. No one has succeeded in producing him successfully on Broadway, but in being rejected by the timid snobbery of Times Square he is in excellent company. And there is no doubt that he can by-pass the taboos of the market, and reach a wide contemporary audience in free Europe and the Americas.

Lorca's theater-poetry fulfills many of the prescriptions of Yeats and Eliot, but it is strongly marked by his unique genius, his rare combination of talents. And it is nourished by the Spanish tradition, which was showing new vitality just before Franco put out the light. These matters are already clear in his early play, *The Love of Don Perlimplín for Belisa, in His Garden. Don Perlimplín* is a romantic farce, slighter and lighter than his most famous pieces, *Blood Wedding* and *The House of Bernarda Alba,* but it is a small masterpiece. When he wrote it he was already in control of his difficult art.

The story is old, lewd and rather savage: that of the old man married to a lusty young wife, one of the standard situations of neoclassic farce. But Lorca, without losing sight of the farce, lifts it to poetry also, and poetry of power and freshness. This he accomplishes in four swift scenes; and to understand his art it is necessary to think over this sequence in some detail.

In the first scene we see Don Perlimplín, a studious type on the dark side of middle age, dressed in a white wig and dressing gown, in his study. His old servant Marcolfa is telling him that it's time he got married, so that when she dies he will have a wife to take care of him. Marriage, says Marcolfa, has great charm, hidden delights; and at that moment we hear Belisa offstage singing a song of shameless childish eroticism. Marcolfa leads Don Perlimplín upstage to the window; we look out with him, and see Belisa on her balcony across the way, very lightly clad. Don Perlimplín gets the point of this vision: Belisa is white inside, like sugar, he says; would she strangle me? Belisa's mother appears, and between her and Marcolfa Don Perlimplín finds himself betrothed to Belisa. The mother is one of those terrible cold-hearted eighteenth-century duennas; she reminds her daughter with speed and clarity that money is the foundation of happiness, and Don Perlimplín has money. The scene ends with Don Perlimplín firmly committed, and trembling with a mixture of terror and delight, like a boy when the possibilities of sex first touch him.

The second scene shows Don Perlimplín's bedroom on the wedding night. In the middle of the stage is a huge ornate bed, and there are six doors, one to the rest of the house, the others giving on to five balconies. First we see Don Perlimplín, magnificently dressed, receiving final instructions from Marcolfa. They disappear and Belisa enters in ruffled negligee, singing to offstage guitar music. After a brief scene between her and Don Perlimplín—who says that she is like a wave of the sea—two sprites draw a gray curtain across the stage, concealing Don Perlimplín, Belisa, and the bed. These sprites giggle and chatter with the inhuman merriment of little girls of twelve or thirteen, say—bright-eyed, heartless, knowing little creatures, as children are when they are full of shrewd curiosity but not yet seasoned by any human experience. Presently they open the curtain and depart. Stage and bed are flooded with bright sunlight coming through the five opened doors to the balconies, the iron church bells of the city are banging for matins, and Don Perlimplín is sitting up in bed beside the sleeping Belisa, with a great pair of horns on his head, decorated with flowers. Belisa, when she lazily wakes, admits nothing,

87

but Don Perlimplín sees five hats under the five balconies which show that five men have visited her during the night. Lorca has thus exaggerated the farcical situation of the old man and his young wife; but the combination of bright light, loud iron bells, and big ornate horns adds pity and terror to the scene. When Belisa wanders off to get dressed, Don Perlimplín is left sitting alone on the edge of the bed, and he sings a beautiful lyric on the theme that love has mortally wounded him.

The third scene shows Don Perlimplín and Marcolfa. Marcolfa is deeply ashamed for her master, and moreover she reports that Belisa has already become infatuated with a sixth man. Don Perlimplín is delighted to hear it. He tells the weeping Marcolfa that she understands nothing, and brusquely sends her away. Belisa enters dreamily, mulling over the new young man, whom she has seen, from whom she has received letters, but whom she has never talked to. Don Perlimplín catches her in this daydreaming, tells her that he understands everything, that (being old) he is beyond mortal life and its ridiculous customs, and that he will sacrifice himself for her and her new love.

The final scene is Belisa's rendezvous with the young man, in the garden, at night. First we see Don Perlimplín and Marcolfa, she more grieved than ever, Don Perlimplín more crazily inspired. He tells Marcolfa that tomorrow she will be free, and that then she will understand everything; this bit feels like a farewell. When they go we hear offstage singing, and Belisa enters in her most glamorous finery. She sings a serenade in alternation with the offstage voices. Don Perlimplín meets her, and assures himself that she loves the young man better than she has ever loved before, better than her own body. He tells her that in order that she may have the young man forever, he will kill him—and he runs off, drawing his dagger. Belisa yells for a sword to kill Don Perlimplín: but at that moment the young man, his head wrapped in a scarlet cape, a dagger in his breast, staggers in mortally wounded. Belisa pulls off the cape, revealing Don Perlimplín, who dies. He has just time to explain that this was the triumph of his imagination; he had made Belisa fall in love with the lover he invented. So he gave her a new and deeper knowledge of love, made a new woman of her, as Marcolfa explains at the end: gave a human soul, at last, to the beautiful body. It is Belisa's initiation into love's mystery, corresponding to Don Perlimplín's initiation in the first scene.

The poetic effect of this sequence is intense and direct, but Lorca gets it out of a combination of very old and traditional elements.

Thus there is the basic situation of the old man and the young wife, which in baroque Continental comedy, or on the Restoration stage in England, is usually treated in the hearty, simple-minded mode of broad farce. Cervantes wrote a brilliant interlude of this kind called *The Jealous Old Man*, in which the fun is based on the disharmonies of human physiology, and the audience is expected to sympathize solely with the triumphant wife. Lorca expects us to remember that worldly old theme, and he emphasizes both its theatricality and its ancient, classic quality in the characters, their language, and their costumes. Don Perlimplín in his white wig and scholarly dressing gown; Marcolfa in the striped dress of the stage servant; Belisa's mother with her great wig full of beads and ribbons and stuffed birds; and Belisa herself, the sharp essence of the amoral female: this cast of characters is made to seem as old as nightmare, almost eternal.

But just because the farce and its people seem so ancient, it strikes us as not only farcical but also sinister. Lorca, while keeping the cynical old tale, with its neo-classic stagy glitter, also views it in the perspective of a later, gloomier, and more romantic age; he transposes it to bring out also the love-death theme. That theme also is traditional in European literature, as Denis de Rougemont explained in his book, *Love in the Western World*.

89

He traces the terrible aspiration beyond physical love to some of the Provençal poets, and he thinks that the love-death theme which re-echoes through the nineteenth-century literature obscurely revives the heretical cult of the Cathari. Lorca certainly seems to echo the theme here with a full sense of its deep roots, especially in Don Perlimplín's lyric on the mortal wound of love, and in the final scene in the garden, which has the ceremonious-ness of the dark old erotic rite.

It is an extravagant notion to combine farce and *Liebestod*, but Lorca knew that it was extravagant. It is by means of the *style* of the piece that he makes an ac-ceptable fusion of such disparate elements; for a know-ing style implies the limitations of mood and viewpoint which the author has accepted in advance, and thus makes them acceptable and comprehensible to the audience. Lorca indicates the style of his play in its sub-title: "An Erotic Alleluya." An alleluya is something like a valentine: a love poem decorated with pictures, gilt cutouts, lace paper, and the like; something heroic, over-done, absurd: an *extravagant* offering to the beloved. All the elements of the production, music, sets, costumes, acting, should obey the requirements of this style. And one must remember that it is a Spanish style, akin per-haps to those drawings and paintings of Goya's— wounded cavaliers, frightening mustachioed old women, greedy young women in discreet mantillas—in which the remains of eighteenth-century elegance are seen in a somber light.

Though this play is so unlike anything in English, it is a species of poetic drama. And it achieves much that Yeats and Eliot sought with only partial success. They were both lyric poets first and dramatists second; and both tended in their early efforts to approach poetic drama as though it were an overgrown type of lyric. Yeats's early plays have the Yeatsian lyric melody, but lack the tensions, the contrasts, and the varied move-ment of drama. Eliot's *Murder in the Cathedral* and

Family Reunion sound like his lyrics considerably diluted. Eliot felt that himself, as he has explained; but his usual diagnosis of the trouble is that he has not discovered the right verse form for the stage. He proposes to solve the problem by working out the proper versification. To Eliot's experiments, and to his immense authority, we owe the notion that the problem of poetic drama in our time is simply that of finding a type of verse which will work onstage. And many young poets proceed as though drama could somehow be deduced from the lyric by further exploration of the properties of verse.

Lorca also was a lyric poet before he succeeded on the stage, and his lyric verse shows (like that of Yeats and Eliot) the all-pervasive *symboliste* influence. He is an authentic poet, even by the exigent standards of our masters. But from the first he drew also upon the resources of the old and popular Spanish tradition of balladry: his first collection is entitled *Romancero Gitano,* "Gypsy Balladier." And the ballad is a far more promising clue to drama than the "pure" *symboliste* lyric, precisely because it typically suggests a story: a situation, contrasted characters, a significant event. The *symboliste* lyric, on the other hand, owes its purity to its source in the single feeling of the isolated poet. It is very difficult to derive from it the sense of separate but interacting lives; the movement of real change; the significance of a deed or an event: in short, the objectivity of drama, which is founded (however indirectly) upon sympathy and perception. We must simply recognize, I think, that the inspiration, the poetic point, of the *symboliste* lyric is not dramatic, while that of the ballad is.

It is clear that the whole conception of *Don Perlimplín*—the gentle, absurd, heroic old man; the animal-beauty and her mother; the weepy servant, the struggle with love's cruelty—struck Lorca as poetic. The narrative sequence is itself poetic, like that of the ballads we know. One can conceive a ballad version of *Don Perlimplín,* but not a *symboliste* lyric which would really capture the theme. Thus in trying to get the poetry of the play one must consider not only the passages in verse, beautiful though they are, but the movement of the play as a whole. The poetry is in the characters and their relationships, in the conception of each of the four scenes, and especially in the sharp but quickly resolved contrasts between them. Cocteau's formula applies exactly to *Don Perlimplín:* "The action of my play is in images, while the text is not: I attempt to substitute a 'poetry of the theater' for 'poetry in the theater.' Poetry in the theater is a piece of lace which it is impossible to see at a distance. Poetry of the theater would be coarse lace; a lace of ropes, a ship at sea. . . . The scenes are integrated like the words of a poem." Thus the poetic effect of *Don Perlimplín* strikes us most sharply in the transitions from one scene to another: from Don Perlimplín's study to the glamour and music of the wedding night; from the childish chatter of the sprites to Don Perlimplín's humiliation in the morning. And as soon as we feel the poetry in the whole sequence, Lorca's prose has its poetic effect as well as his music and his visual scheme. Lorca is such a virtuoso of the theater that he can use and control all of its resources to present his poetic vision.

Yeats and Eliot began with verse rather than with the theater, but both of them felt the need of a story and a form which should make the play itself (as distinguished from the language) poetic. And both sought these elements in myth and ritual. Yeats proceeded from Irish myths, to an English version of *Oedipus,* to forms based on the *Noh* play; Eliot experimented with Greek myths and with adaptations of Christian ritual forms. These experiments have proved to be extremely suggestive, and it may well be that they still have much to teach us. But they seem to show, among other things, that it is very difficult to reincarnate a myth in our time. Myths as we read them in learned collections tempt us with their suggestion of deep poetic insights; but the crucial labor of the dramatic poet, faced with the modern stage and the modern crowd, only begins at that point. So many have failed—either relapsing into cultishness or antiquarianism, or reducing the myth to an abstract and pseudophilosophical scheme—that the very word "myth" has ceased to be respectable. Yet the problem remains; and in its most general form it is probably the heart of our difficulty with poetic drama.

It is this problem which *Don Perlimplín* solves quite naturally and directly. If the story is not strictly a myth, it has the qualities our poets seek in myth: it seems much older and much more generally significant than any history which is literally true; yet Lorca does not seem to have thought it up, but rather to have perceived it, or heard it, in the most intimate chamber of his sensibility. In embodying it on the stage he is careful to preserve this oft-told feeling, like song, or a tale told by a grandmother. This he does with the utmost confidence and simplicity. He is sustained by the knowledge that he is talking about things which other artists have seen before in his Spanish tradition; for Don Perlimplín seems to come from the same world—which we now see is still alive—as Don Quixote and Goya's frightening people.

Because the story has this "mythic" quality, its basic form is quite naturally that of ritual or traditional ceremony. The first scene is a betrothal, and we are made to feel that it has been celebrated countless times before, and will be endlessly again: it is the first stage of the initiation into love's cruel mystery; for the old man is as virginal as a boy. The second scene (a kind of interlude in the movement of the piece) is not a ritual; but the third scene, a wedding night with all the pomp of music and costume, is conceived as a sinister epithalamion, moving with decorum toward its predestined pathos. The final scene in the garden, with its serenade in antiphonal form, its symbolic suicide, its cult of love as death, is the place where Lorca's feeling for the ancient heretical love rites that De Rougemont studies is most

93

unmistakable. It is there that Belisa, in her turn, is "initiated." I do not know how consciously Lorca worked all this out; he has the authentic artist's sophistication of feeling combined with philosophical reticence. But I am sure that the ceremonious quality of these scenes (like a duel or a bullfight) must be carefully observed in production, for it is their decorum which gives the underlying passion its cutting edge.

It has been said (notably by Mr. Roberto Sanchez in his valuable book on Lorca) that Lorca is a theatrical rather than a truly dramatic talent. He does not, for example, have Ibsen's moral and intellectual drive, and he rarely deals directly with contemporary scenes or contemporary issues. He usually finds the clue to a play in painting, or music, or poetry, or even in the theater itself. In all his work (as in *Don Perlimplín*) he relies on stage effects to carry much of the burden. And in these respects his art is akin to that of some modern masters of theatrical style, directors and designers, who do not so much create drama as interpret it in the theater. Mr. Sanchez has a point, but I think he somewhat misinterprets the evidence.

He is thinking of men of the theater like Reinhardt or Copeau, who seem to have had some more or less direct influence upon Lorca. Reinhardt was famous for his allusive and learned experiments with style—doing *Midsummer Night's Dream* as romantic music, playing about with expressionism, or the baroque, or the Commedia dell'Arte. And it is true that each of Lorca's plays is, among other things, a self-conscious period piece. *Doña Rosita* is founded upon the sweet faded conventions of the turn of the century. It is like a delicately tinted family picture in a velvet frame, a provincial keepsake smelling of lavender and Spanish Victorianism. Even *Blood Wedding* and *Yerma*, for all their power and violence, owe something to painting or balladry. This habit of starting with art may seem perilously close to orchestrating Bach, a substitute for real creation—or even to the next step:

the ads for diamonds or perfume, in which certain tricks of French painting are used to produce snob appeal. Lorca in fact does have a fondness for play, self-conscious virtuosity, even chic; but this does not bother me as much as it does Mr. Sanchez. The theater, when it has the proper gusto, often feeds upon itself and the other arts in this way, but without sacrifice of original dramatic content. Lorca's theater accomplished this, I think. The limitations which Mr. Sanchez feels in his art are not those of the merely clever, arty theatrical interpreter, but those of an artist who, in our fragmented and polyglot culture, stays within the idioms of one national culture. When a national culture revives, its art forms seem significant, filled with immediately relevant moral and spiritual content; and that seems to have occurred in Lorca's Spain. When that happens, the theater, in its play with images from art, may be allusive without being merely arty.

The House of Bernarda Alba, the play which Mr. Sanchez regards as the best dramatically, is interesting in this connection. Mr. Sanchez thinks it a powerful picture of contemporary Spanish provincial life, with the qualities of the best modern realistic drama. Lorca himself calls it a photograph; and according to people who know the country, he has achieved a surface accuracy comparable to Ibsen's or Chekhov's. But it would be a mistake to take its realism too straight: the label "photograph," like the label "alleluya" on *Don Perlimplín,* indicates the very self-conscious style, which alludes to a whole context of meaning. *Bernarda Alba* is a period piece like the others; it utilizes the conventions of nineteenth-century realism with the same kind of sophisticated intention as that with which *Don Perlimplín* utilizes its more ancient conventions. The blankness of the photograph is part of the composition which includes the severe character of Bernarda herself, and the deathly white walls within which she strives to hold her myopic vision steady.

In this problem of Lorca's restaging of Spanish art we must remember the analogies between forms of art and forms of human life. They are most evident in old countries with whose art and literature we are familiar. One may feel it even on revisiting New England: the white clapboards, the old ladies, the slender elms still seem to be "right out of the pages" of Whittier or Hawthorne. The Paris taxi drivers still argue à la Molière; the hard-bitten concierges in cheap hotels are still imitating Balzac. And the Spanish mark on art and character is one of the deepest. I have never been to Spain, but I have seen Sancho Panza and his burro in northern New Mexico, and the faces of old people reflecting (even at a distance of thousands of miles and many generations) the subtle faces in Spanish painting. Perhaps the natural role of the artist in a living culture is to make these forms, with the changes which time brings, visible and significant again.

But Lorca was unusually fortunate in being able to work with such fertility within his native culture; it is a commentary on our rootless state, in which all the familiar forms of life and art begin to seem vague and irrelevant, that his riches should seem somehow against the rules. It is growing harder and harder in our time for a writer to stay within one traditional culture. Yeats was hardly content with his Irish revival beyond youth. Our own Southern writers hesitate painfully between the South, where their roots are, and the national scene in which they are obliged to live, almost as ill-defined as the rest of us.

The deeply Spanish nature of Lorca's art does not prevent it from speaking to us. His sense of history—"the masquerades which time resumes"—is very modern; in his ability to mingle the most contradictory perspectives in one composition, and to shift with sureness from the pathetic to the farcical-frightening, he is in the class of our favorite poets. And he writes poetry of the theater as our poets would like to do. We cannot use his Spanish language, or the symbolic language of the moral and esthetic forms of his tradition. But we can learn to read it, and to discover thereby an authentic modern poetic drama.

T. S. Eliot's *Poetry and Drama**

In this lecture, as Mr. Eliot explains, he is taking stock, asking himself what he thinks of poetry and drama now, after more than thirty years of writing both criticism of drama and plays of his own. His essays are always good reading because they are so well written, even when (as in some of his earlier pieces) he makes only one or two small points. In this lecture the plot has thickened: he is considering Shakespeare, Yeats, Synge, Maeterlinck; at the same time he is not unaware of what he had to say about some of those writers years ago; and in addition to that he is assessing his own experiences in writing *Murder in the Cathedral*, *The Family Reunion* and *The Cocktail Party*. The result is one of his most brilliant performances: he has never been more agile, urbane, and cautious.

As a critic, Mr. Eliot is first of all a master and a connoisseur of lyric verse. His usual practice, especially in his earlier work, is to *assume* the poetry, and then by means of careful discriminations, and very apt quotation, to present a single sharp, suggestive insight, which stimulates his readers to further reading of their own. This gives him the air of knowing far more than he is willing to say. He addresses his audience (which is in

* *Poetry and Drama*, by T. S. Eliot, Harvard University Press, 1951.

dire need of instruction) with candor and courtesy, but rather mistrustfully; for he never forgets his responsibilities, to himself, to his readers, and to the poetic mystery of which he is the hierophant. It is essential to this method to be very gingerly about all general questions, "to halt," as he said very early, "at the borders of metaphysics." Thus he very seldom considers the form and structure of a whole poem, to say nothing of more general questions still—the subject of this lecture, for example. His great success as a critic has been due both to his practical familiarity with verse-writing, and to his ascetic regime as a prose-writer. Under his influence a whole generation has been anxiously exploring versification, metaphor, the use of irony and ambiguity, and the whole fascinating lore of the lyric poet's use of the English language. But drama is not the same art as lyric poetry; in drama the synthesis of incidents, characterization, and more or less concealed thought underlie the arts of language. And the question is, to what extent has Mr. Eliot's long preoccupation with drama increased his understanding of that art, and modified his practice as a critic?

In general, it seems to me that Mr. Eliot is coming, though very reluctantly, to see that drama is a different art from lyric poetry, and that it cannot therefore be understood as merely a special instance of versification. He is much more disposed now than he was thirty years ago to look beneath the language of drama to the action (the *"moto spirital"*) of the characters, from which their words come. This tendency is very evident if one compares his remarks on *Hamlet* in this lecture with the famous essay on that play which he published in 1919. But as his understanding of drama has deepened, his preoccupation with "practical playwriting" has increased; and the lessons he has learned from the entertainment industry, as revealed in his plays and what he says about them, confuse and even contradict his growing sense of what poetic drama might be at its best.

In considering his own plays, Mr. Eliot does not mention *Sweeney Agonistes,* which I regret, because that play, or fragment, remains the most powerful and promising piece he has written for the stage. He starts with *Murder in the Cathedral.* He regards it as a success, on the whole, given the special occasion and the limited purpose for which it was written. He modestly points out that the subject is remote enough to be acceptable as "poetic," and that the church audience was willing to be piously bored, yet capable of being surprised. But he explains that, for him, the play was a dead end, just because of its special subject and occasion. In writing it he solved none of the general problems of poetic drama in our time. A style—which, at that time, still meant for him chiefly a kind of versification—was still to be found; a style capable of reaching the unregenerate general public, and of dealing with a contemporary theme.

In *Family Reunion* he resolutely tackled these problems: took a contemporary story and setting; diminished the role of the chorus (which is so important in *Murder in the Cathedral*) and above all brought his verse as close as possible to colloquial speech. He is still pleased with the verse: "What I worked out," he says, "is substantially what I have continued to employ: a line of varying length and varying number of syllables, with a caesura and three stresses." He believes that the first act is good, and that the diminution of the chorus's role was a step in the right direction; but on the whole he now dislikes *Family Reunion.* Its comparative failure led him to try to take the question of *dramatic* form more seriously: "In retrospect, I soon saw," he tells us, "that I had given my attention to versification at the expense of plot and character." And he decided that "the deepest flaw of all was in a failure of adjustment between the Greek story and the modern situation." At this point in the story of his adventures Mr. Eliot seems to tremble on the verge of a real understanding of poetic drama, as distinguished from the versified play. But he does not attempt to explore his insights any further. Instead he turns to the more immediate, superficial, and pressing problem of putting himself across on the contemporary stage at all; from the deeper strategy of his development as a dramatist, to tactics; in short, to the making of *The Cocktail Party*.

In devising *The Cocktail Party* he resolved, to begin with, to have "no chorus and no ghosts." He again used a Greek story—that of Euripides' *Alcestis*—but transformed it so completely that no one but himself has recognized Reilly, the convivial psychiatrist and good-natured Christian, as Herakles' spiritual heir. It was necessary to his conception of poetic drama that the play be in verse, but as he explains, "I laid down for myself the ascetic rule to avoid poetry which could not stand the test of strict dramatic utility: with such success, indeed, that it is perhaps an open question whether there is any poetry in the play at all." In this passage he seems to imply a distinction between verse and poetry, but not to suspect that there might be any poetry in the drama itself.

Mr. Eliot says that he is still exploring the weaknesses of this play, and perhaps his critics should emulate him in this respect, and not try to estimate *The Cocktail Party* until it has had time to sink in. But on the evidence of the Broadway performance and this account of its genesis, *The Cocktail Party* looks to me like the momentary triumph of Mr. Eliot's ingenuity over his poetry. Just because of this ingenuity the play is fascinating to watch, as a good mystery-thriller is. But the mystery, or puzzle, is the author's: how will Mr. Eliot bootleg his Christian message into our unsuspecting show shops? As for the play onstage—the play between the characters— it is thin, patchy in style, and unconvincing. The first act moves amusingly enough, on the serviceable principles of parlor comedy; but compared with virtuoso-pieces of this kind—with *Private Lives*, for example—it is pedestrian and creaky. If the second act were to succeed as a play, we should have to be able to take the characters and their problems seriously; for this act purports to show the conversions, or changes of heart, of three suffering human creatures. This we do not see; but we do begin to discern the philosophy, or moral, of the tale, and its emergence is interesting to watch. The third act is the weakest: we are in another clattering (though somewhat discouraged) cocktail party with the same characters; and the sensational results of sanctity, with which the story ends, are reported over the martinis. The conception of this act seems to have some of the sardonic savagery of *Sweeney Agonistes;* but the characters, their actions, and their language are colorless and abstract— there is none of Sweeney's nightmare intensity in it.

If one thinks over the series of Mr. Eliot's plays, one is inevitably reminded of Henry James's adventures in practical playwriting. It is true that Mr. Eliot has certain gifts which James lacked, especially an intellectual inclusiveness which augurs well for his success. There is something theatrical and entertaining about the play of his fine mind even in his soberest critical essays; and if he continues in the direction indicated by *The Cocktail Party* he may invent a superior form of intellectual entertainment, akin to Shaw's, but more theologically and philosophically sophisticated. But if one takes his completed plays as a series of efforts to make a commercially viable poetic drama, what they have to teach us is James's melancholy lesson all over again: it is necessary to eliminate the cargo in order to save the ship; the medium of the entertainment industry is too light to sustain much poetry. *The Cocktail Party* floats in the near-vacuum of Times Square more triumphantly than *Murder in the Cathedral,* but it carries far less poetry and far less drama.

But Mr. Eliot's understanding of poetic drama is not limited to his tactics as a practical playwright. On the contrary, it appears to be deepening, at the same time that his plays grow thinner. At the end of his lecture he summarizes his understanding of the lost art of poetic drama in a passage which shows very clearly how far that understanding now reaches:

I should not like to close, however, without attempting to set before myself, and, if I can, before you, though only in dim outline, the ideal toward which it seems to me that poetic drama should strive. . . . It seems to me that beyond the namable, classifiable emotions and motives of our conscious life when directed toward action —the part of life which prose drama is wholly adequate to express—there is a fringe of indefinite extent, of feeling which we can only detect, so to speak, out of the corner of the eye and can never completely focus; of feeling of which we are only aware in a kind of temporary detachment from action. There are great prose dramatists—such as Ibsen and Chekhov—who have at times done things of which I would not otherwise have supposed prose to be capable, but who seem to me, in spite of their success, to have been hampered in expression by writing in prose. This peculiar range of sensibility can be expressed by dramatic poetry, at its moments of greatest intensity. At such moments we touch the border of those feelings which only music can express. We can never emulate music, because to arrive at the condition of music would be the annihilation of poetry, and especially of dramatic poetry. Nevertheless, I have before my eyes a kind of mirage of the perfection of verse drama, which would be a design of human action and of words, such as to present at once the two aspects of dramatic and musical order.

In this crucial passage Mr. Eliot means by "action," not Dante's *moto spiral*, which refers to every mode of the spirit's life, in response to every "range of sensibility," but only physical movement or outward deeds. This is the realm which he assigns to "dramatic order," and all the rest to "musical order." By "music" he seems to mean, at this moment, Plato's unheard *musiké*, which I take to be another word for "poetry" in the widest sense. In other places he uses "music" more narrowly, to mean the art which uses the medium of sound only; but the word in that use would make no sense here. What he seems to be saying, therefore, is that the art of drama itself is not a form of poetry; it cannot be poetic without verse. As long as he holds that view he will, I think, fall short of an adequate conception of poetic drama. He will not know what to do with Ibsen and Chekhov, or, for that matter, the prose passages in Shakespeare. And when he considers the arts of plotmaking and characterization and *dianoia* he will be at the mercy of the engineers of the well-made play, who agree with him about the realm of drama because, with their myopic positivism, they recognize no other realm of human experience at all. In all of this we must recognize the struggles of the lyric poet to understand drama as a branch of his art, instead of lyric verse as merely one of the resources which great dramatists can use for their wider purposes. His acceptance of drama is thus still incomplete; yet in thirty years he has come a long way; and his lecture, like all his work, offers us the exhilarating spectacle of a mind struggling with basic mysteries, and so always alive, changing, and instructive.

Boleslavsky's *The First Six Lessons**

THIS is the book which Mr. Boleslavsky's admirers have
been wishing for for some years—or rather the first book,
since it is no more than an introduction to his theater
lore. Anyone who has been so fortunate as to come into
contact with his teaching (which says so much more to
us than many of his American productions) understands
that Mr. Boleslavsky has a great deal to give. And we
must be grateful to Mrs. Isaacs (who writes an introduction) and to the National Theatre Conference, for
finally getting *The First Six Lessons* into print.

Mr. Boleslavsky entered the Moscow Art Theatre more
than twenty years ago, and so was able to learn from the
greatest actors and directors of that group when it was
at its height. At that time the theater and the opera in
Moscow and St. Petersburg must have been flourishing
in a way which we can hardly imagine in this country.
There were not only the great state-supported institutions for music, drama and the dance, there was a wealth
of private permanent theaters, devoted to every kind of
entertainment, from music hall to Ibsen. The Russian
cities were theatrical centers for all Europe; Mr. Boleslavsky never tires of recalling the performances of Duse
and Salvini. In reading *The First Six Lessons* it is neces-

* *Acting: The First Six Lessons*, by Richard Boleslavsky,
Theatre Arts, Inc., 1933.

sary to remember this background, for the actor's education which Mr. Boleslavsky outlines implies, I think, his
native performer's paradise. When he asks the neophyte
to study music, painting, and dramatic literature, it
sounds grotesque to us, who remember our favorite talkie
star. Mr. Boleslavsky understands the situation of the
American actor, yet I think he looks back to Tsarist Moscow as the norm. One must remember also that as a
writer Mr. Boleslavsky belongs to the generation immediately following Chekhov. The Chekhovian farewells
are still ringing in his ears; and if, as Director of the
First Studio, he reacted against the drama of leisure-
class weariness and nostalgia, it was only toward home-
sickness grown democratic: tears and *sensibilité* for the
masses. The present book is in the form of a dialogue
between Mr. Boleslavsky and "The Creature"—a young
actress who applies for lessons. I am sorry to say that
the Creature is such a quivering bundle of smiles and
tears and lovable childish fits of anger that it is impossible for me, and perhaps for the present generation in
general, not to be embarrassed by her. It is too much like
Dickens' joyous weeping; Mr. Boleslavsky is a great
lover of Dickens.

Only when one has discounted Mr. Boleslavsky's
rather awkward writing in a taste which is at least quite
foreign to us, does it become possible to appreciate the
importance of his book. And this is a pity, for the Six
Lessons constitute the elements of an important technical
treatise on the theater. They are devoted respectively to
Concentration, Memory of Emotion, Dramatic Action,
Characterization, Observation and Rhythm. They are
based on an elaborate and very wide conception of the
theater, but they are essentially the outline of a technique of acting, and so can be thoroughly understood
only by one who is actually engaged in trying to act.
Mr. Boleslavsky indicates this fact by placing the lessons months or years apart in the life of his actress pupil.
Yet they have much to say to anyone who is trying to

learn any related art, and even to the mere reader of poetry or drama. But the quality of the book may best be illustrated by a few quotations.

Here is a paragraph from the lesson on Concentration, which is the introduction to the course: "In a creative theatre the object for the actor's concentration is the human soul. In the first period of his work—the searching —the object for concentration is his own soul and those of the men and women who surround him. In the second period—the constructive one—only his own soul. Which means that, to act, you must know how to concentrate on something materially imperceptible—on something which you can perceive only by entering deeply into your own entity. . . . In other words you need a spiritual concentration on emotions which do not exist, but are invented or imagined." This is corrected by the following, from Dramatic Action: "First you want something, it is your artist's will; then you define it in a verb, it is your artist's technique; and then you actually do it, it is your artist's expression." Having come thus far, in your working on a part, "You could take a pencil and write 'music of action' under every word or speech, as you write music to lyrics for a song; then on the stage you would play that 'music of action'. . . . You would have to memorize your actions as you memorize the music. You would have to know distinctly the difference between 'I complained' and 'I scorned' and, although the two actions followed each other, you would be just as different in their delivery as the singer is when he takes 'C' or 'C flat'."

These observations may sound elementary; yet for lack of an understanding of such elements most plays one sees are a disorganized mush. If you take a good play and try to distinguish the "actions" underneath the words, you will soon see how fundamental, and how far from obvious, these technical suggestions are. The same method may be used in reading poetry. The Metaphysicals yield much to an attack of this kind; Eliot's most "incomprehensible" pieces become clearer if you try to make them out thus dramatically, and Mr. Eliot reads them aloud in this way. One is even tempted to say that the difference between good and bad poetry is the difference between poetry in which the "actions" are clearly distinguished and poetry in which they are all blurred together in one inorganic mood.

The method which Mr. Boleslavsky preaches was, I have been told, founded on the Chekhovian drama; yet it is always pointing away from any kind of naturalism toward the artistic effort itself. In Characterization we read:

The Creature: But Emotions must be characterized just as clearly as body and mind. What is the proper way to do that?

I: When you have mastered the general human emotions in the part . . . When you know when and why anger comes, or pleading, sorrow, joy or despair, whatever the case demands, when it is all clear to you, start to look for one fundamental quality: freedom in expressing your emotions. Absolute, unlimited freedom and ease. That freedom will be your characterization of the emotions at hand.

In the last lesson Mr. Boleslavsky offers a tentative definition of Rhythm: "The orderly, measurable changes of all the different elements comprised in a work of art—provided that all those changes progressively stimulate the attention of the spectator and lead invariably to the final aim of the artist."

These quotations are of course not intended as a description of the method of training. Those who are interested will explore the book itself. But I should like to try to summarize the gist of it as given in this book. Mr. Boleslavsky begins with the "five senses," exercises in seeing, hearing and feeling things which do not exist, and seeing, hearing or feeling them so clearly as to make the audience share the experience. He then proceeds to the memory of emotion, which is the source of the actor's "emotions which do not exist"; his "golden box," his palette, in the realm which Proust came to regard as more real than the world of common sense. Dramatic Action, which Mr. Boleslavsky discusses next, is the framework of the role or of the play. The "dramatic action" of a play or of a part is always expressed by an infinitive. For instance, the "action" of Chekhov's *The Three Sisters* has been called "to get to Moscow." When Aristotle defines tragedy as the imitation of a completed action he must mean something like this by *action*. The "action" of Oedipus in *Oedipus the King* is not the story which is unfolded in the course of the play, but "to get at the cause of the city's woes"—a movement which reaches its completion in the full revelation of his guilt. As for the "action" of this play—for each play as well as each role has an "action"—that is very hard to find in a masterpiece of a remote epoch, but the quest is very fruitful.—These three elements are the core of the technique; the "five senses," memory of emotion, and "action." It will be noticed that it all applies to the "soul," or part of the soul, and that it might easily be erected into a kind of pseudoreligious exercise. Training in voice, body and diction, which is almost the whole thing in most American dramatic schools, is here used merely as a means to an end. One gathers that the great theaters of Tsarist Russia, secular monasteries, with prolonged novitiates and high priests of histrionics, dance and song, were in fact spiritual outgrowths of and perhaps substitutes for the Church. That was an age of great performers, though not of great drama. The training which Mr. Boleslavsky has to offer is torn out of this context; and the question becomes urgent, what place has this training with us?

When Mr. Boleslavsky first came to this country Mrs. Herbert K. Stockton founded the American Laboratory Theatre and made him director. He was director for about six years, with Broadway interludes; produced perhaps fifteen plays, and commenced the training of several hundred students of acting. The interest of this experiment will readily be granted by anyone who sees possibilities in the technique and is dissatisfied with what the reviewers call our "show shops." Such people however are rare, and most of them have their own irons in the fire. The few who enjoy either good plays or good performances would rather go to Mei Lan-fang or Chaliapin when they come to town; to visiting foreign groups for good plays, or to Harlem for tap-dancing and vaudeville—than watch an earnest young group trying to act. And who will blame them? Most students of a dramatic school assemble in the hope of a stage success: diction, cold cream, a penthouse in the Village and a sunburn from Tia Juana. Even the few who may be converted to grander ideas soon begin to long for the places where the audiences are; and who can blame them for that?—in Russia one could have both. The necessity of choosing plays which must seem good to persons of various tastes and backgrounds (Moscow to Kalamazoo) and which one may yet hope will "draw" is another source of confusion. That the Laboratory Theatre survived as long as it did and commanded the enthusiasm of a number of hopeful novices (including the present writer) is an indication of the extraordinary qualities of its founder, and also of Mr. Boleslavsky's personal charm, his great gifts as a teacher, and the fascination his lore holds for anyone with any kind of designs on the theater.

Mr. Boleslavsky is now in Hollywood, his interlocutor is a movie actress as well as a creature. He gives his present credo in answer to the Creature's complaints about the talkies: "The only thing you have to do is to march abreast of the times and do your best—as an artist."

One may see how Mr. Boleslavsky, who is in his every breath or gesture a pure being of the theater, could take no other course. And one may still hold that the best Mr. Boleslavsky has to offer will never take in the commercial theater. Who would squander years of devotion on *Ice-bound* or *Mourning Becomes Electra?* Who would try for a Broadway success through a laborious training when it is so obvious that success is usually achieved there through other methods? The only possible reason for studying Mr. Boleslavsky with care is to acquire skill in drama, acting or perhaps poetry. At present these good things are very rare and very lost on the American stage. I can imagine trying to disengage the essence of Mr. Boleslavsky's teaching from its accidents, which are due to the fact that he is strictly an interpretive artist of a particular age, and then applying it to various studies. I can even imagine a small group of self-confessed amateurs making a hobby of the theater under Mr. Boleslavsky's guidance; enjoying the plays for their own sake, acting them for each other and maybe an infrequent audience. At this time no scorn need be felt for an amateur theater: if Mr. O'Neill writes for the Guild, Seneca wrote for the parlor. And there are plenty of contemporary plays, dramatic experiments, adaptations of the classics, which could only be cultivated by such a group.

Meanwhile the fact that Mr. Boleslavsky can issue Six Lessons from Hollywood is a matter for rejoicing, both for him and for his readers.

PART II

Shakespeare

Macbeth as The Imitation of an Action

I PROPOSE to attempt to illustrate the view that *Macbeth* may be understood as "the imitation of an action," in approximately Aristotle's sense of this phrase.

The word "action"—*praxis*—as Aristotle uses it in the *Poetics*, does not mean outward deeds or events, but something much more like "purpose" or "aim." Perhaps our word "motive" suggests most of its meaning. Dante (who in this respect is a sophisticated Aristotelian) uses the phrase *moto spiral,* spiritual movement, to indicate *praxis.* In Aristotle's own writings *praxis* is usually rational, a movement of the will in the light of the mind. But Dante's *moto spiral* refers to all modes of the spirit's life, all of its directions, or focuses, or motives, including those of childhood, dream, drunkenness, or passion, which are hardly rationalized at all. When using Aristotle's definition for the analysis of modern drama it is necessary to generalize his notion of action in this way, to include movements of the spirit in response to sensuous or emotionally charged images, as well as consciously willed purpose. But this seems to me a legitimate extension of the basic concept; and I do not think it does real violence to Aristotle's meaning.

Aristotle, in his *Psychology* and his *Ethics,* as well as

in the *Poetics*, and Dante, in the *Divine Comedy*, seem to imagine the psyche much as an amoeba looks under the microscope: moving toward what attracts it, continually changing direction or aim, and taking its shape and color from the object to which it is attached at the moment. This movement is "action"; and so we see that while the psyche is alive it always has action; and that this changing action in pursuit of real or imagined objects defines its mode of being moment by moment.

When Aristotle says that a tragedy is the imitation of an action, he is thinking of an action, or motive, which governs the psyche's life for a considerable length of time. Such an action is the quest for Laius's slayer in *Oedipus Rex*, which persists through the changing circumstances of the play. In this period of time, it has a beginning, a middle, and an end, which comes when the slayer is at last identified.

I remarked that action is not outward deeds or events; but on the other hand, there can be no action without resulting deeds. We guess at a man's action by way of what he does, his outward and visible deeds. We are aware that our own action, or motive, produces deeds of some sort as soon as it exists. Now the plot of a play is the arrangement of outward deeds or incidents, and the dramatist uses it, as Aristotle tells us, as the first means of imitating the action. He arranges a set of incidents which point to the action or motive from which they spring. You may say that the action is the spiritual content of the tragedy—the playwright's inspiration—and the plot defines its existence as an intelligible *play*. Thus, you cannot have a play without both plot and action; yet the distinction between plot and action is as fundamental as that between form and matter. The action is the matter; the plot is the "first form," or, as Aristotle puts it, the "soul," of the tragedy.

The dramatist imitates the action he has in mind, first by means of the plot, then in the characters, and finally in the media of language, music, and spectacle. In a well-written play, if we understood it thoroughly, we should perceive that plot, character, and diction, and the rest spring from the same source, or, in other words, realize the same action or motive in the forms appropriate to their various media.

You will notice that this is a diagrammatic description of the perfect play, perfectly understood. Therefore one cannot hope to illustrate it perfectly, even in the case of a play like *Macbeth*. *Macbeth*, however, does impress most of its readers as having a powerful and unmistakable unity of this kind: the plot, characters, and imagery all seem to spring from the one inspiration. It is that strong and immediately felt unity which I rely on—and upon your familiarity with the play. Not that I am so foolish as to suppose I grasp the play completely or that I could persuade you of my view of it in these few minutes. All I can attempt is to suggest the single action which seems to me to be the spiritual content of the play, and illustrate it, in only a few of its metaphors, plot devices, and characterizations.

The action of the play as a whole is best expressed in a phrase which Macbeth himself uses in Act II, scene 3, the aftermath of the murder. Macbeth is trying to appear innocent, but everything he says betrays his clear sense of his own evil motivation, or action. Trying to excuse his murder of Duncan's grooms, he says,

The expedition of my violent love [for Duncan, he means]
Outran the pauser, reason.

It is the phrase "to outrun the pauser, reason," which seems to me to describe the action, or motive, of the play as a whole. Macbeth, of course, literally means that his love for Duncan was so strong and swift that it got ahead of his reason, which would have counseled a pause. But in the same way we have seen his greed and ambition outrun his reason when he committed the murder; and in the same way all of the characters, in the irrational darkness of Scotland's evil hour, are compelled in their action to strive beyond what they can see by reason alone. Even Malcolm and Macduff, as we shall see, are compelled to go beyond reason in the action which destroys Macbeth and ends the play.

But let me consider the phrase itself for a moment. To "outrun" reason suggests an impossible stunt, like lifting oneself by one's own bootstraps. It also suggests a competition or race, like those of nightmare, which cannot be won. As for the word "reason," Shakespeare associates it with nature and nature's order, in the individual soul, in society, and in the cosmos. To outrun reason is thus to violate nature itself, to lose the bearings of common sense and of custom, and to move into a spiritual realm bounded by the irrational darkness of Hell one way, and the superrational grace of faith the other way. As the play develops before us, all the modes of this absurd, or evil, or supernatural, action are attempted, the last being Malcolm's and Macduff's acts of faith.

In the first part of the play Shakespeare, as is his custom, gives us the intimate feel of this paradoxical striving beyond reason in a series of echoing tropes and images. I remind you of some of them, as follows.

From the first Witches' scene:

> When the battle's lost and won. . . .

> Fair is foul and foul is fair.

From the "bleeding-sergeant" scene:

> Doubtful it stood;
> As two spent swimmers that do cling together
> And choke their art. . . .

So from that spring whence comfort seem'd to come
Discomfort swells. . . .

Confronted him with self-comparisons
Point against point rebellious, arm 'gainst arm. . . .

What he hath lost noble Macbeth hath won.

From the second Witches' scene:

> So fair and foul a day. . . .

> Lesser than Macbeth, and greater.

> His wonders and his praises do contend
> Which should be thine or his. . . .

> This supernatural soliciting
> Cannot be ill, cannot be good. . . .

> . . . nothing is
> But what is not.

These are only a few of the figures which suggest the desperate and paradoxical struggle. They are, of course, not identical with each other or with outrunning reason, which seems to me the most general of all. But they all point to the "action" I mean, and I present them as examples of the imitation of action by means of the arts of language.

But notice that though these images themselves suggest the action, they also confirm the actions of the characters as these are shown in the story. The bleeding sergeant, for instance, is striving beyond reason and nature in his effort to report the battle—itself a bewildering mixture of victory and defeat—in spite of his wounds. Even the old King Duncan, mild though he is, is caught in the race and sees his relation to Macbeth competitively. "Thou art so far before," he tells Macbeth in the next scene, "That swiftest wing of recompense is slow/To overtake thee." He then races Macbeth to his castle, whither the Messenger has outrun them both; and when he arrives, he is at once involved in a hollow competition with Lady Macbeth, to outdo her in ceremony.

I do not need to remind you of the great scenes preceding the murder, in which Macbeth and his Lady pull themselves together for their desperate effort. If you

think over these scenes, you will notice that the Macbeths understand the action which begins here as a competition and a stunt, against reason and nature. Lady
Macbeth fears her husband's human nature, as well as
her own female nature, and therefore she fears the light
of reason and the common daylight world. As for Macbeth, he knows from the first that he is engaged in an
irrational stunt: "I have no spur/To prick the sides of my
intent, but only/Vaulting ambition, which o'erleaps it-
self/And falls on the other." In this sequence there is also
the theme of outwitting or transcending time, an aspect
of nature's order as we know it: catching up the consequences, jumping the life to come, and the like. But this
must suffice to remind you of the Macbeths' actions,
which they paradoxically understand so well.

The Porter scene has been less thoroughly studied as
a variation on the play's main action. But it is, in fact,
a farcical and terrible version of "outrunning reason," a
witty and very concentrated epitome of this absurd
movement of spirit. The Porter first teases the knockers
at the gate with a set of paradoxes, all of which present
attempts to outrun reason; and he sees them all as ways
into Hell. Henry N. Paul[*] has explained the contemporary references: the farmer who hanged himself on the
expectation of plenty, the equivocator who swore both
ways to commit treason for God's sake. When the Porter
has admitted the knockers he ironically offers them lewd
physical analogies for outrunning reason: drink as tempt-
ing lechery into a hopeless action; himself as wrestling
with drink. The relation of the Porter to the knockers is
like that of the Witches to Macbeth—he tempts them
into Hell with ambiguities. And the inebriation of drink
and lust, lewd and laughable as it is, is closely analogous
to the more terrible and spiritual intoxication of the Macbeths.

Thus, in the first part of the play both the imagery

[*] See *The Royal Play of Macbeth*, Macmillan, 1950.

and the actions of the various characters indicate or "imitate" the main action. Aristotle says the characters are imitated "with a view to the action"—and the Porter, who has little importance in the story—is presented to reveal the action of the play as a whole in the unexpected light of farcical analogies, contemporary or lewd and physical.

Before I leave this part of the play I wish to point out that the plot itself—"the arrangement or synthesis of the incidents"—also imitates a desperate race. This is partly a matter of the speed with which the main facts are presented, partly the effect of simultaneous movements like those of a race: Lady Macbeth is reading the letter at the same moment that her husband and Duncan are rushing toward her. And the facts in this part of the play are ambiguous in meaning and even as facts.

These few illustrations must serve to indicate how I understand the imitation of action in language, character, and plot in the first two acts of the play. Macbeth and his Lady are embarked on a race against reason itself; and all Scotland, the "many" whose lives depend upon the monarch, is precipitated into the same darkness and desperate strife. Shakespeare's monarchs do usually color the spiritual life of their realms. And we, who remember Hitlerite Germany, can understand that, I think. Even Hitler's exiles, like the refugees from Russian or Spanish tyranny, brought the shadow to this country with them.

I now wish to consider the action of the play at a later stage, in Act IV, scene 3. This is the moment which I mentioned before, the beginning of Malcolm's and Macduff's act of faith, which will constitute the final variation on "outrunning reason." The scene is laid in England, whither Malcolm and Macduff have fled, and it immediately follows the murder of Macduff's wife and child. Like the exiles we have known in this country, Macduff and Malcolm, though in England, have brought Scotland's darkness with them. They have lost all faith in reason, human nature, and common sense, and can therefore trust neither themselves nor each other. They are met in the hope of forming an alliance, in order to get rid of Macbeth; and yet under his shadow everything they do seems unreasonable, paradoxical, improbable.

In the first part of the scene, you remember, Malcolm and Macduff fail to find any basis for mutual trust. Malcolm mistrusts Macduff because he has left his wife and child behind; Macduff quickly learns to mistrust Malcolm, because he first protests that he is unworthy of the crown, to test Macduff, and then suddenly reverses himself. The whole exchange is a tissue of falsity and paradox, and it ends in a sort of nightmarish paralysis.

At this point there is the brief interlude with the Doctor. The king's evil and its cure and the graces which hang about the English throne are briefly described. Paul points out that this interlude may have been introduced to flatter James I; but however that may be, it is appropriate in the build of the scene as a whole. It marks the turning point, and it introduces the notion of the appeal by faith to Divine Grace which will reverse the evil course of the action when Malcolm and Macduff learn to outrun reason in that way, instead of by responding to the Witches' supernatural solicitations as Macbeth has done. Moreover, the Doctor in this scene, in whom religious and medical healing are associated, foreshadows the Doctor who will note Lady Macbeth's sleepwalking and describe it as a perturbation in nature which requires a cure beyond nature.

But to return to the scene. After the Doctor's interlude, Ross joins Malcolm and Macduff, bringing the latest news from Scotland. To greet him, Malcolm clearly states the action, or motive, of the scene as a whole: "Good God, betimes remove/The means that makes us strangers!" he says. Ross's chief news is, of course, Lady Macduff's murder. When he has gradually revealed that, and Macduff and Malcolm have taken it in, accepting some of the guilt, they find that the means that made them strangers has in fact been removed. They recognize themselves and each other once more, in a sober, but not nightmarish, light. And at once they join in faith in their cause and prepare to hazard all upon the ordeal of battle, itself an appeal beyond reason. The scene, which in its opening sections moved very slowly, reflecting the demoralization of Malcolm and Macduff, ends hopefully, with brisk rhythms of speech which prepare the marching scenes to follow.

This tune goes manly. . . .

> Receive what cheer you may:
> The night is long that never finds the day.

The whole scene is often omitted or drastically cut in production, and many critics have objected to it. They complain of its slowness, of the baroque overelaboration of Malcolm's protests, and of the fact that it is too long for what it tells us about the story. All we learn is that Malcolm and Macduff are joining the English army to attack Macbeth, and this information could have been conveyed much more quickly. In the first part of the play, and again after this scene, everything moves with the speed of a race; and one is tempted to say, at first, that in this scene Shakespeare lost the rhythm of his own play.

Now, one of the reasons I chose this scene to discuss is that it shows, as does the Porter scene, the necessity of distinguishing between plot and action. One cannot understand the function of the scene in the whole plot unless one remembers that the plot itself is there to imitate the action. It is then clear that this scene is the peripeteia, which is brought about by a series of recognitions. It starts with Malcolm and Macduff blind and impotent in Macbeth's shadow and ends when they have gradually learned to recognize themselves and each other even in that situation. "Outrunning reason" looks purely evil in the beginning, and at the end we see how it may be good, an act of faith beyond reason. The scene moves slowly at first because Shakespeare is imitating the action of groping in an atmosphere of the false and unnatural; yet we are aware all the while of continuing speed offstage, where

> each new morn
> New widows howl, new orphans cry, new sorrows
> Strike heaven on the face. . . .

The scene is thus (within the rhythmic scheme of the whole play) like a slow eddy on the edge of a swift current. After this turning, or peripeteia, the actions of Malcolm and Macduff join the rush of the main race, to win. I admit that these effects might be hard to achieve in production, but I believe that good actors could do it.

Shakespeare's tragedies usually have a peripeteia in the fourth act, with scenes of suffering and prophetic or symbolic recognitions and epiphanies. In the fourth act of *Macbeth* the Witches' scene reveals the coming end of the action in symbolic shows; and this scene also, in another way, foretells the end. The last act, then, merely presents the literal facts, the windup of the plot, long felt as inevitable in principle. The fifth act of *Macbeth* shows the expected triumph of Malcolm's and Macduff's superrational faith. The wood does move; Macbeth does meet a man unborn of woman; and the paradoxical race against reason reaches its paradoxical end. The nightmare of Macbeth's evil version of the action is dissolved, and we are free to return to the familiar world, where reason, nature, and common sense still have their validity.

To sum up: my thesis is that *Macbeth* is the imitation of an action (or motive) which may be indicated by the phrase "to outrun the pauser, reason." I have tried to suggest how this action is presented in the metaphors, characters, and plot of the first two acts; and also in the peripeteia, with pathos and recognitions, the great scene between Malcolm, Macduff, and Ross.

I am painfully aware that these few illustrations are not enough to establish my thesis. Only a detailed analysis of the whole play might do that—and such an analysis would take hours of reading and discussion. But I think it would show that Aristotle was essentially right. He had never read *Macbeth,* and I suppose if he could he would find Shakespeare's Christian, or post-Christian, vision of evil hard to understand. But he saw that the art of drama is the art of imitating action; and this insight, confirmed and deepened by some of Aristotle's heirs, can still show us how to seek the unity of a play, even one which shows modes of the spirit's life undreamed of by Aristotle himself.

Measure for Measure*

I suppose that in our efforts to understand Shakespeare, what we seek is a grasp of his plays as plays. We want his theater to come fully alive before us; we wish to hear and to understand as fully as possible the complex harmonies which we now believe are there.

Forty or fifty years ago a kind of "higher criticism" of Shakespeare was in vogue, which had the effect of disintegrating the plays and obscuring or denying their coherence. The corruption of the texts was emphasized, and Shakespeare's authorship was questioned in whole or in part. His dramaturgy was compared, to his disadvantage, with Ibsen's. His psychology, when it did not seem to agree with modern notions, was dismissed as faulty or irresponsible. When Shaw proclaimed that Shakespeare lacked *his* up-to-date enlightenment he merely confirmed a widespread prejudice. The spirit in which we now read Shakespeare seems to me much healthier. We are less in love with our own clichés; less sure of our psychological insight; less fascinated with the well-made plot, and more interested in the culture of the Renaissance and the Middle Ages, which, at the very least, provided Shakespeare with indispensable *means* to his great work. And so we are able, once more, to accept

* A lecture given at Harvard University, March 22, 1951, for the Department of English.

126

him as a still-living master of the theater and of the lore of the human psyche; and we assume that the ultimate purpose of our scholarship and criticism is rather to learn from him than merely to learn *about* him.

Measure for Measure is one of the plays which has suffered most from the habit of judging Shakespeare on extrinsic grounds, and it is one of the plays which has benefited most from our new awareness of his perennial wisdom and artistry. For this reason it is not in the least original to say (as I propose to do) that *Measure for Measure* has a great deal to offer us. Nevertheless it is still puzzling, for it is not exactly like anything else which Shakespeare wrote. Is it a kind of morality play, like *Everyman?* Is it a problem play, or a thesis-play, as Mr. W. W. Lawrence suggested? Or what kind of composition is it?

My general thesis is that it is to be understood as both philosophy and poetry-of-the-theater, but that the two are not separate, or merely mechanically combined, but two cognate modes of presenting a single underlying vision of man in society. But, if so, then the philosophy must be something quite unlike our contemporary academic philosophy. And the poetry-of-the-theater is not what we usually mean by poetry, for our conception of this art is derived from the modern lyric, the lyric since Baudelaire perhaps; and we know that our best lyricists distrust all the uses of the mind but the lyric inspiration itself. Shakespeare's philosophy and theatricality emerged from another tradition—one which tends to be lost to sight—and in approaching *Measure for Measure* we must remember a little of what that tradition contained.

I begin with a few remarks on the nature of the "philosophy" in this play.

The Duke, in his first speech, which begins the play, says to Escalus,

Of government the properties to unfold
Would seem, in me, to affect speech and discourse.

The Duke in fact will not unfold the properties of government in speech and discourse alone. But the play which follows, when the Duke has disappeared and Angelo is ruler, will unfold them, both dramatically and in the dialectic of Angelo, Isabella, and Lucio. The Duke, as Friar, will observe and explain this unfolding, and in the last act, having resumed his authority as Duke, he will demonstrate the same philosophy of government and its properties in the trials and judgments of all the characters.

The title of the play suggests the mystery of human government which the drama explores in one way and the philosophy in another: that of the relation between Justice and Mercy, or Charity. "Measure for Measure" may mean either weight for weight, an eye for an eye and a tooth for a tooth, or it may mean a measure of measurement itself: that is, Charity, which measures or proportions the strict justice of human reason seeking mathematical rigor.

The late Theodore Spencer, and more recently Mr. Tillyard, has shown that in Shakespeare's time the medieval tradition, with its combination of Greek thought and Christian religion, was still very much alive. Mr. I. A. Richards has pointed out many echoes of Platonic philosophy in Shakespeare's plays, notably in *Troilus and Cressida*. These and other writers have made it clear that, whatever Shakespeare may have read or believed, this complex philosophic heritage was somehow available to him and to the cultivated part of his audience. If one looks at the *Basilikon Doron* of James I—whom some believe to have been the model for the Duke—one can see that the monarch was thinking about justice and mercy, spiritual and temporal authority, and indeed all the properties of government, with the same philosophic background as we find in *Measure for Measure*.

In attempting to understand the philosophy in this play, therefore, one must remember the classic formulations, both Greek and Christian, which were then current. Mr. G. Wilson Knight, in his fine essay, interprets the play as a straight allegory of New Testament morality. There is no doubt that this element is there, and extremely important. St. Paul's distinction between Mosaic Law, with its rational and literal justice, and the new rule of Charity (or Mercy, as the Hebrew prophets put it) pervades the play. But so, I think, does the Platonic and Aristotelian philosophy of society, which is based upon the analogy between the body politic and the individual, whose life has many modes, vegetable, animal, rational, and whose body has many organs serving the whole in different ways. Because this philosophy recognizes the diversity of man in a social whole, it produces an *analogical* conception of justice, which is almost as far from Mosaic literal and univocal justice as Charity itself is. This Greek tradition was essential in building that central, catholic philosophy of government which Shakespeare's contemporaries—James himself, Hooker—were endeavoring to oppose to the rationalized revolutionary and counterrevolutionary movements of the time: to Puritanism, to Jesuitism, and in a later generation to the single-minded absolutism of a Hobbes. Thus "the nature of our people and our city's institutions," as the Duke puts it, are the very matter of the play's philosophy. In the mirror of the Duke's "Vienna," and in the light of the Greek-Christian tradition, the play reveals the actual drama of government in Shakespeare's own city.

If these observations are acceptable, it follows that the philosophy in this play is not a theory, or a neat system of logically connected concepts, but *philosophia*, the love of wisdom. This love of wisdom, embodied in the order of society and in the literary heritage, had been fed by a tradition going back through the Middle Ages and St. Augustine to the Greeks and to the Bible. And so Shakespeare can use the ancient formulations as commonplaces, *topoi*, means or occasions for communicating his own view of the perennial mystery.

Mr. W. W. Lawrence called *Measure for Measure* a "problem comedy." He was thinking of the contemporary play of ideas or theses, of Ibsen, Shaw, even Brieux. He was, however, not very happy with this comparison, and no wonder, for it is of the essence of our problem plays that the central wisdom is lacking, and, therefore, that the theses of the reformers are all the thought they have to offer. Shakespeare has no thesis, no "platform," in that sense—he leaves that kind of thinking to his Angelos and his Isabellas. He is not, in fact, solving a problem so much as he is setting forth, from many points of view, an ineluctable mystery in human affairs.

It is only philosophy in the ancient sense of *philosophia* which can come from the same sources of insight as narrative, character, poetry-of-the-theater. And it is only a sophisticated version of poetry-of-the-theater which can recognize the source it may have in common with the love of wisdom. I proceed to a few observations on this knowing theatricality as Shakespeare used it.

Everyone knows that Shakespeare made his plays out of histories, stories, and even other plays. *Measure for Measure* is made from the story and the play of Promos and Cassandra, to which Shakespeare added the traditional bed-trick, which has offended so many, and the ancient theme of the ruler who (like Harun-al-Rashid) visits and observes his people in disguise. All of these tales were old and familiar, and, as many writers have pointed out, such old familiar tales had been accepted since the Middle Ages as having some sort of meaning or truth, some light to throw upon human nature and destiny. They constituted a sort of secular mythology for Renaissance Europe; and for Shakespeare they provided, like the philosophic themes in *Measure for Measure*, themes or topics or commonplaces of another kind. It was his practice to combine, vary, and develop them to make the rich texture of his stage play.

The philosophic themes of *Measure for Measure* are

to be found in the structure of the play, in the discourses
of the Duke, and in the dialectic of Angelo, Isabella and
Lucio. The debates reveal Shakespeare's familiarity with
Renaissance-Aristotelian logic and rhetoric, as Sister
Miriam Joseph has shown. The narrative themes, on the
other hand, are developed dramatically by the players.
Shakespeare uses the situations and the main events of
the old stories very much as exercises in good acting
schools, in which the actors are taught to improvise
plays on situations given by the instructor. Thus, given
the departure of the Duke and the new authority of
Angelo, what will happen? The players will show us,
making-believe the given characters and situations, and
following out with full concentration and consistency the
terrible or pathetic results. In short, the traditional tales
which Shakespeare used were publicly acceptable means
whereby his players could "hold the mirror up to
nature."

If one thinks of Shakespeare's stories in this way,
one can, I think, understand their apparent artificiality.
Would Lear, really, have given his kingdom away to his
daughters? Would the Duke really have embarked on
that romantic project of departure and return in disguise? I do not know; but I see that in each case the
initial situation is the basic *donné*, or call it the working
hypothesis, of the whole play. The significance is to be
found (as in an experiment in the laboratory) in the
working out of the vital results of this made-believe situation. And I am sure that the very *arbitrariness* of this
basic *donné* is essential: it establishes that concrete,
fated, unrationalizable element in human affairs without which there can be no actual life and no drama.
Because Shakespeare had these accepted tales, with all
their inexplicable concreteness, he had a means of reflecting the intimate actuality of human life before or
beneath all theory.

Thus I think that the philosophizing and the playing
in *Measure for Measure* spring from the same source,

show the same "habits of mind and feeling," and embody the same cultivated awareness of man in society. I should say that the style of the play as a whole was at once rational and poetic. But this is a style with which we are not very familiar, in contemporary drama or literature, and to understand it one must think of a very few masters, high points in the tradition, who had attained a comparable balance and flexibility.

I have already mentioned Plato. The dialectic in the great dialogues does not move toward the univocal concept; it is not resolved by deciding between two contradictory propositions, but by the appearance of a new insight, which transcends and in a way includes both sides. In this process the characters, and their interplay, are as important as the play of concepts; and when an anecdote or a parable is introduced, we do not feel that the subject is being changed, but rather that it is being presented in a complementary way. The whole is sustained and lightened by a spirit of play or significant make-believe, which we feel both in the actions of the characters and in the hypotheses to be discussed. I feel a similar sophisticated and resourceful style in the central cantos of the *Purgatorio,* where Vergil and Marco Lombardo expound the traditional philosophy of man in society, the issues of justice and mercy, of temporal and spiritual authority, against the darkness of anger and the darkness of Italian policies, which Dante and Marco so sharply recall. In such works, as in *Measure for Measure,* we are invited to play the poetry and the philosophy off against each other, illuminating the actual tangle of human affairs with wisdom, yet never losing the distinction between the general truths of philosophy and the concrete realities of life.

But this is more than enough by way of general observations. I now wish to suggest a reading of the play. For this purpose I shall follow one thread only in the complex pattern, that of the role of the Duke.

The Duke has displeased many critics, who report either that he is not a character at all, but merely a *deus ex machina*, or else that he is a liar, weakling and hypocrite. The Duke is puzzling, and perhaps ultimately not quite successful. But it is certain that he is the center of the play, and the clue to its intention and its peculiar style. Shakespeare did not find him in the Promos-Cassandra play, but added him, to give that old story a new form and meaning. He made the Duke both a character within the play who takes a crucial part in the struggle, and at the same time a sort of stage director, who because of his power and wisdom can start and control the action as though from the wings. It is a question whether we can accept this double function, and believe in the Duke both within and above the story. But at least we may investigate the theatrical and philosophic purpose of such a creation.

Let us consider first his character within the story, that of the eccentric Duke of Vienna. W. W. Lawrence (who on the whole takes the play pretty literally) points out that he represents the authority of both Church and State, as he plays Friar and Duke. He thinks that he is a conventional figure, especially at the end of the play, when, like many a prince or priest, he winds up the plot and points the moral. This conventional element is there, no doubt, but we must remember how lively the issues of spiritual and temporal authority were in the early years of James I's reign; even in the playhouse they must have meant more than a romantic convention. James himself took his responsibility as guide and leader of his people with pedantic seriousness. He would have agreed with Marco Lombardo that both spiritual and temporal rulers have the duty of showing the people *della vera cittade almen la torre*, "at least the tower of the true city." The Duke is such a ruler: he wishes to *teach* Vienna the properties of government. That is the clue to his action in the play, and also to his *régisseur's* action outside the play: he wishes to show London the properties of government in the experimental situation of Vienna.

If the Duke is understood as a teacher, his supposed deviousness and hypocrisy is explained, for he is a very modest and empirical kind of teacher. He would understand the force of Plato's or St. Augustine's dicta, that a teacher can only help the student to realize what he knew already. He anticipates our progressive educators, who maintain that one can really learn only "by doing." Mr. Donald Stauffer (in *Shakespeare's World of Images*) describes the Duke's pedagogical style as follows:

The Duke of dark corners sets a number of problems as experiments which various characters must work out for their own salvation. The Duke prefers the laboratory to the lecture-room. Shakespeare returns to his conviction that experience is the best teacher, that painful experience may be deliberately intensified in order to assure a clearer acknowledgment of error; that realization, remorse, repentance, and a change of heart are unavoidable steps in moral betterment.

When the Duke departs and leaves Angelo in charge, he sets the city a practical problem in government. The city unfolds the properties of government by trying all the wrong moves; and the Duke is at hand to reinforce the painful lessons in his counsel to Isabella or to Claudio, and at last by the order which, as temporal ruler, he can impose. In all of this, his role is a figure and an analogue of that of Shakespeare, who set up the situation of the old Promos-Cassandra story, guided its development, and interpreted it in the light of his own traditional philosophy of government.

Most students of *Measure for Measure* find the first three acts the best. It is there that we most unmistakably recognize poetry, drama, the natural movement and variety of life as in Shakespeare's greatest tragedies. And it is there that the Duke takes the least active part. Having set the stage for a tragedy by handing his city over to the tyrannical perfectionist Angelo, he merely observes, and explains in secrecy to the characters whose suffering might bear fruit in wisdom.

Shakespeare and the Duke clearly intended this effect, as the first part of their demonstration. They wished to show to Vienna, and to London in the mirror of Vienna, a tragedy in the making: a city hopelessly divided between the doctrinaire perfectionism of Angelo and Isabella, the innocent sensuality of Claudio, and the cynical sophistication of Lucio, the whole placed against a background of the weaknesses, fears and darkness of routine human nature as we see it in any corrupt old city. The nascent tragedy which results is wonderfully suggestive for us also. I see in it a theme like Yeats's "The centre cannot hold,/Mere anarchy is loosed upon the world." The Duke, with his wisdom and power, represents the missing center. Angelo and Isabella, with their ambitious intellectuality, represent revolutionary or counterrevolutionary forces, which change their policies but not their narrow power drives, as they struggle in the dark and empty center. Of course the debates are in the theological terms of Shakespeare's time, but our contemporary tragedies of the dissolving center are strikingly similar in their *dramatic* form.

In this nascent tragedy Lucio is the counterpart of the Duke, and thus throws a great deal of light upon him. Lucio has a talent for chaos as great as the Duke for wisdom or the central order. Shakespeare uses Lucio in the first two acts as the chief reflector of the action, to use Henry James's valuable term: it is through Lucio's intelligent and faithless eyes that we grasp what is going on. In Act I, scene 2, he explains the first impact of Angelo's inhuman strictness upon the easy-going and corrupt humanity of Vienna, with bawdy wit spiced with theological learning. He bids us appreciate the poetry in which Claudio, on the way to execution, expresses his plight:

> Our natures do pursue,
> Like rats that ravin down their proper bane,
> A thirsty evil, and when we drink we die.

"If I could speak so wisely under an arrest I would send for certain of my creditors," says Lucio, with urbanity. And it is he who both appreciates and dismisses Isabella, the green novice, when he hails her as "a thing ensky'd and sainted." The image is, I think, that of the plaster saint. Isabella feels it a mockery, and the mockery is deepened through the implicit contrast with Julietta, whom Lucio next describes in the beautiful lines,

> As those that feed grow full, as blossoming time
> That from the seedness the bare fallow brings
> To teeming foison, even so her plenteous womb
> Expresseth his full tilth and husbandry.

Above all, it is Lucio who arranges the fight between Angelo and Isabella, and interprets it for us, blow by blow, with the most refined psychological insight. It was his inspiration to "bait the hook with a saint in order to catch a saint," as Angelo says, with terror, when he sees how he is caught. He suggests that Lucio is more than the devil's advocate, almost the devil himself.

At the end of the play Lucio is the only character whom the Duke cannot really forgive. Shall we say that Lucio has insight without integrity? Or that he represents treachery, which Shakespeare, like Dante, hates above all other sins? Or that he is only a trimmer like Rosencrantz and Guildenstern, a "private of fortune," neither for good nor for evil but only for his trivial self? However that may be, Lucio has things his own way in the first half of the play, encouraging the unregenerate appetites of all the characters, using his imagination in the service of darkness, while the Duke keeps his true power hidden. But in the middle of Act III the Duke begins to take an active part, and thenceforth Lucio is out of his depth and can no longer interpret the action for us. The tragedy is arrested on the very brink of catastrophe, and the end of the play presents the mystery of justice and mercy in a way undreamed of in Lucio's philosophy.

Readers of *Measure for Measure* who like the first three acts usually dislike the last two, when the Duke asserts his authority to restore order. They miss the completion of the tragic sequence as we find it in *Macbeth* or *Hamlet* or *Othello*. In the fourth act, in those great works, evil both triumphs and ends: Othello caves in under Iago's lies, Macbeth and his lady taste the fruit of futility and fear, Claudius's regime breaks up in scandal and confusion. In the fifth act the vision of evil is complete against a good which is implicit or announced as coming. In *Measure for Measure* the Duke arrests the course of evil and presents the good, or the order of wisdom, more directly and at length. So we are balked of our tragedy; but do we get an adequate ending to the play in a different key?

The Duke starts to intervene when he proposes the bed-trick to Isabella. In Act IV his plans proceed with great speed. The timing is close, and the language is prose, as though Shakespeare by this change of rhythm, this sudden deflation and sobriety in speech, were warning us that playtime is over, the citizens have been given their head long enough, and now we must pay attention to matters of a different kind of seriousness. I find this change of key successful: there is poetic power in the sequence in the prison, at night, with the Duke working against time to avert catastrophe and accept his sober responsibility for his flock. But the act is very brief, a modulation from the nascent tragedy of the first three acts to the complex demonstration of Act V. Just before abandoning his role as Friar, the Duke warns us what to expect in the final part of his play: "By cold gradation

and well-balanced form," he says, "we shall proceed
with Angelo."

It has often been maintained that Act V is a mere
perfunctory windup of the plot, in which Shakespeare
himself had no real interest. I am sure that on the contrary it is composed with the utmost care, and in perfect
consistency with the basis of the whole play—this quite
apart from the question whether one *likes* it or not. It is
indeed so beautifully composed that it could almost
stand alone. Perhaps we should think of it as a play
within a play, presenting the theme of justice and mercy
in another story and in another and colder tone. But the
new story—that of the Duke's intervention and demonstration—was implicit from the first; and the new cold,
intellectual tone may be understood as underneath the
more richly poetic manner of the first three acts.

We are invited to watch this last act with a kind of
double vision: from the front of the house, and at the
same time from the wings, where we can see the actors
getting ready to pretend to be what they are not. For,
like the Duke, we know what they are; and moreover
we have seen the Duke's backstage preparations for the
final play. This final public play, unrolling before us and
the supposedly ignorant Duke, is in the form of a series
of trials. The first begins with Isabella's desperate com-
plaint of Angelo, and ends when her suit is rejected on
the basis of the evidence then publicly available: the
wild improbability of her story, and Angelo's fine reputation and dignified manner. The second trial starts when
the Duke leaves Angelo and Escalus to try Isabella for
her supposed lying slander, and it ends when the Duke
returns in his Friar disguise as a witness, and is suddenly
revealed as the Duke when Lucio pulls off his hood. The
third part ends both trials: the Duke, now revealed as
both judge and witness, metes out justice to all, but on
the assumption which we know to be false, that Claudio
is dead. Notice that up to this point the trials and judgments have obeyed the strictest reasoned conception of

justice, and the facts insofar as they could be found under the frightened and passionate lies in which they had been hidden. The Duke has been following a Mosaic regularity, and he has also been acting like that image of justice as a woman with bandaged eyes, a pair of scales in one hand and a sword in the other. He had been pretending to rely, not upon his concrete vision, but upon reportable "facts" and his abstract measuring-machine. But in the final act of this playlet the Duke as it were drops the bandage from his eyes, confesses what he can really see, starting with the fact that Claudio is alive. He then tempers or proportions justice with mercy, abstract reason with his perception of the analogical relationships between real people, in whom truth and error, sin and grace, are mingled in ways which mathematics cannot compute.

I offer this sketch of Act V, not as exhausting its complexities, but to support my view that it is composed with the greatest care and the most self-conscious art. But some of its critics say that it is not poetry, not the proper end of a poetic drama, but only philosophy or abstract allegory. And indeed it is certain that when the Duke establishes an order in accordance with his own wisdom, we have a new relation between the dramatic and philosophic developments of the theme of justice and mercy.

Thus it is possible to read this act as an allegory of the descent of Mercy upon the scene of human judgment. The Duke, like God, comes not to destroy the Law—for he uses it to demonstrate everyone's guilt—but to transcend it. His role throughout the play is like that of Grace, in its various forms, as theologians describe it: he works through the repentant Mariana and Claudio to illuminate their motives and prevent their follies; and here at the end he answers Mariana's prayer after the intercession of Isabella. These relationships are worked out with theological scrupulousness, and I suppose that

Shakespeare must have been aware of the possibility of this interpretation.

But at the same time he presents the Duke, not as God or as a mere symbol of a theological concept, but as a real human being; and Act V may be read, therefore, as the end of a *drama*. Mariana's love for Angelo had sharpened her insight: she was able to see through his actual savagery to the bewildered spirit within, which still had the potentialities of good; and the Duke, as Friar, had encouraged her in this strength, charity and understanding. Isabella had a wise *doctrine* from the first, but this doctrine remained helpless and disembodied until she was matured by suffering and appealed to by Mariana. In short, the play has shown how the wisdom of love proceeded from the Duke to the two women, to be finally confirmed by him when they reveal it at the end. Such is the *drama* of the growth of wisdom in Vienna, which finally reverses the tragic course toward anarchy. Angelo sees it coming, as knowledge of the truth, before Mercy supervenes; he is caught and stopped in his tracks as by a sudden glare of light:

> I should be guiltier than my guiltiness
> To think I can be undiscernible
> When I perceive your Grace, like power divine,
> Has look'd upon my passes.

Dante's Vergil has a phrase which accurately describes such a growth of understanding in human terms: "Love kindled by virtue," he says, "always kindles another, if only its flame shows outwardly." Vergil is of course a pagan, and he is thinking of the relationships between himself, Statius, and Dante, whose love was shown outwardly in their writings. The point is that Shakespeare's eye, as usual, was upon the reality of human experience, where the life of drama is.

Moreover, he has written Act V with its own theatrical poetry, which one may miss if one does not think of its actual stage effects. It is not only a series of trials and a demonstration of the Duke's wise authority; it is also a masquerade, a play of pretense and illusion. As we watch it with what I have called our "double vision," we can see each character in turn compelled to relinquish his pretense, his public costume. And in this respect Act V merely carries to its conclusion one of the important theater-poetic themes of the whole play, that of human life itself as a dream or masquerade. Angelo expresses it when he says,

> . . . my gravity,
> Wherein, let no man hear me, I take pride,
> Could I with boot change for an idle plume
> Which the air beats for vain. O Place! O Form!
> How often dost thou, with thy case, thy habit,
> Wrench awe from fools, and tie the wiser souls
> To thy false seeming!

Isabella echoes this when she calls Angelo "seeming, seeming!" and in her vision of man, "most ignorant of what he's most assured,/His glassy essence." The Duke's great speech to Claudio in prison, "Be absolute for death," plays many variations on this theme, for instance:

> Thou art not thyself;
> For thou exist'st on many a thousand grains
> That issue out of dust. . . .

> . . . thy complexion shifts to strange effects
> After the moon. . . .

> Thou hast nor youth nor age,
> But as it were an after-dinner's sleep,
> Dreaming on both.

In the first three acts we are in the midst of these masquerades; we are moved by their seductive passion and music. In the last act, playtime over, the music changes, the masques are put aside, and we are shown what

Shakespeare evidently regarded as the underlying truth of the human situation.

It is our contemporary habit to believe that "the masquerades which time resumes" (as Eliot puts it) *are* the reality of the human situation. And so the shimmering detail of Shakespeare's theater-poetry is likely to be enough for us; we do not often enquire how it is *composed*, what underlying action governs the form and the movement of the play as a whole. But, because Shakespeare did compose his plays, he must in some sense have seen deeper than the passions, the delusions, the imaginative exuberance which make the incomparable *immediate* life of his theater. He would probably have agreed with Pico della Mirandola about the power and also the danger of Imagination, when not controlled by a deeper vision of the intellect. That is why, in *Measure for Measure,* he can move so freely between theater-poetry and dialectic as two modes of presenting action, the psyche's life. And that, I believe, is why he can present the Duke's demonstration in Act V as the end both of the thought and of the poetic play.

This brings me to my final point, the question of the success of the role of the Duke. Can we accept him, or is he simply too wise and good and powerful to work in a play?

I must admit that I know no simple answer to this question. It would depend upon the innumerable circumstances of a performance; the skill and understanding of the actors, the taste and prejudices of the audience. But I think I see why Shakespeare could have wished to make such a character, who would be both inside the play, and so subject to its fictive situation, and also visible *outside* it, controlling and interpreting its course. He wished to show the *making* of the play at the same time as the play itself. So he presents Vienna, not as literal reporting in the manner of modern realism, but as a significant fiction; and so he modestly and as it were playfully confesses his own authorship, for it is clear that the Duke is a figure of Shakespeare himself. It is a problem in the metaphysics or epistemology of poetry, like that which Dante solved in the *Divine Comedy* by speaking both as author and as protagonist; or like that which Pirandello explores in *Six Characters*.

It may be that Shakespeare solved this problem better in *The Tempest*, where, as G. Wilson Knight remarks, Prospero is lord of the play much as the Duke is in *Measure for Measure*, protagonist and author both. Prospero's art is presented, clearly, from the first, as magic, and that play may be regarded as a consistent though endlessly "true" fairy tale. In *Measure for Measure* Shakespeare's intention was different, perhaps more ambitious; he wished to go farther both in realism and in philosophic thought. If he succeeds, it can only be with a very alert and sophisticated audience.

Professor G. E. Bentley tells me that in his opinion *Measure for Measure* was not written for Shakespeare's usual popular audience, but for some special occasion. He thinks it possible, even probable, that it was written for the Inns of Court, though he adds that there is no real evidence for that. But I eagerly seize on this possibility, and I imagine Shakespeare himself, in the role of the Duke, addressing an audience professionally responsible for the Law. I see him in the Duke's costume, known for the theater man he was, speaking to his learned audience with urbanity and some irony:

The properties of government to unfold
Would seem, in me, to affect speech and discourse . . .

And after this polite gambit, I like to think of him enthralling the lawyers both with his philosophy of government and with the magic of his theater-poetry, lighting his great theme from several sides at once, yet passing it all off easily as his own hypothesis and make-believe.

Two Comedies

SHAKESPEARE'S comedy, both the plays called comedies and the comic passages in the rest of his work, is even harder to understand than his tragedy. The comic in general defies analysis: is there a definition of the laughable, even Bergson's, in which one can have much confidence? Some shrewd observations have been made on particular comedies or writers of comedy, but usually the critics merely prove that every real sense of humor, and even every comic effect, is unique. Molière comes as close as any master of comedy to having a stable point of view, an intelligible convention, and an infallible touch; but it is impossible to reduce all this to a formula. As for Shakespeare, his point of view shifts continually, he employs various conventions in his comedy, and there are many who find his touch far from infallible. Broadway reviewers, who think they know what makes the readers of *The New Yorker* laugh, and antiquarians, who think they know what made the Elizabethans laugh, tend to agree that Shakespeare's comedy is comic no more: here again they clasp hands, with a sophisticated wink, over the safely dead body of our heritage.

If one nevertheless does enjoy Shakespeare's humor, what is the best way to explore its range, learn its habits, assure oneself that one is really getting the point which Shakespeare intended? One method is to keep in mind the fact that Shakespeare wrote to be acted before an audience. One then reflects that laughter in the theater depends upon so many factors—the mood of the audience, what the author has led the audience, in advance, to expect; the rhythm of the performance as a whole; subtleties of timing, attitude, and the like—that it is to be understood and controlled only empirically. Directors and actors know this. Comedians, however talented, have to learn by trial and error how to make audiences laugh at them. Directors often have to experiment with a comic scene, cutting it, changing its timing or business, before they can see how it works. There is every reason to believe that Shakespeare, a practical theater man, worked that way. Starting with an old play or an old story, having in mind a certain company of actors, he wrote his plays in such a way as to control all the elements, and from their combination, before an audience, to get the intended effect of humor or pathos. Each of his comic effects is unique; emerging from the context of the whole acted play, it reflects his sure grasp of the action of *that* play, its comic as well as its pathetic aspects. His sense of humor apparently never sleeps; he reveals it, at will, by manipulating the theatrically perceptible elements which his story provides.

The most ambitious way to learn about Shakespeare's comedy would be to try to produce it. But the opportunity to do that is rare, and an actual production tests many things besides Shakespeare's dramaturgy, notably the skill and talent of the actors, and the moral and physical stamina of the hopeful director. It is an ordeal not to be lightly undertaken. A more practicable (as well as self-indulgent) method is to imagine the ideal performance as one reads the play—not, of course, in all its material details, but as a musician might "hear" a symphony as he read the score. Such a reading of Shakespeare's comedy would, I suppose, turn up much that is obvious; but it might have the value of a prolegomenon: a pedestrian preparation for understanding Shakespeare's comic genius.

The Comedy of Errors and *Much Ado About Nothing* are far from exhausting Shakespeare's comic resources. But they are very different from each other, and by thinking them over together, with an eye to their theatrical point, one may begin to sense the variety and scope of his comic repertoire.

I

Shakespeare took the main story of *The Comedy of Errors* from Plautus's *The Two Menaechmuses*. The basic situation is that of two brothers, identical twins, who were separated in childhood and find themselves by chance in the same city when they are grown; they are so identical that no one can tell them apart. It is very improbable that twins could be so similar that even the wife of one of them couldn't distinguish between them, but Plautus, and Shakespeare after him, calmly assume that identity, and they are right, for this initial absurdity sets the key of the farce to follow. The audience must accept the silly postulate at once; so it is warned to expect, not a fable purporting "truth," but a joke and a tall story.

I do not know why two people who are identical are laughable, but they are, and if they are not only the same height and age and weight, but walk and sit in the same way at the same time, the comic effect is stronger. And if there are more than two, we are still more pleased with them. This principle is well used in the Kaufman-Hart comedy, *Once in a Lifetime,* when twelve movie magnates, the identical Glogauer brothers, march onto the stage in a double-quick procession just before the second act curtain.

Shakespeare must have counted on this property of human identity, for when he devised *The Comedy of*

Errors he provided Plautus's identical twins with servants who were also identical twins. He thus exaggerates Plautus's farcical exaggeration, and is enabled thereby to play many more variations than Plautus could on the plot which may be derived from the basic situation. This situation is the childishly simple one of mistaken identity: every scene in the play is an instance of it; every character in the play is always and only trying to straighten out such a mistake, which the audience always perfectly understands in advance. The most striking quality of this comedy—unique among Shakespeare's plays—is its perfect unity of action, plot and tone. As it quickly unrolls before us it gives the superficial impression of ceaseless movement, variety, and surprise. But that is a matter of great, but essentially mechanical, ingenuity: the play is built like a round, which delights a group of light-hearted singers by piling up and overlapping a single pattern.

It is true that the first scene, in which we see the twins' long-suffering father in trouble, and the last scene, in which father, mother, and the boys are reunited with happy tears, are different in tone from the body of the play: sentimental rather than farcical. But the first scene is a prologue, and the last scene not only brings the intrigue to its happy end, but also serves the essential purpose of changing the mood. Writers of farce have usually some trouble with the end of their fun. There is no inherent reason for halting the perpetual-motion machine of a good farcical plot; the arabesques of absurdity in *The Comedy of Errors* might continue indefinitely, or at least to the limits of the author's ingenuity and the audience's complacency. The plot is wound up neatly and naturally enough by the simple expedient of bringing both sets of twins together, but that is not enough: the postulate—or call it the attitude, or frame of mind—of farce must be broken through; the audience must be relaxed and dismissed in another mood. This may be accomplished in countless ways, but

all who successfully devise farce for the theater feel the
need of this final change of mood. I used to notice that
the old burlesque shows at Minsky's recognized it instinctively. The traveling salesmen would be guffawing
all evening at slapstick, broad jokes, and chorines with
but three crucial rhinestones; but at the end the lights
would soften, the music would slide from the hot,
through the blue, to the frankly old-timy, and a gray-
haired mamma or "mom" would take the center of the
stage to gaze thoughtfully into the electric moonlight.
So the patrons received the whole treatment, gently
eased at last out of their farcical mood into something
warmer, damper and homier.

There is one strand running through the whole
Comedy of Errors which might seem, on a first reading,
to break the mood of farce: the troubled adventures of
Antipholus of Ephesus' long-suffering wife. She is so dis-
turbed when the other Antipholus treats her strangely
that one might think Shakespeare wanted us to share
her tears and frustrations. She and her sister and her
maid, and eventually her real husband's mistress, form a
dreary female procession through the quick twists of the
plot. But I believe that Shakespeare expected us to laugh
at them also, and that, in performance, would be largely
a matter of tempo. The film of a funeral, even, may be
made laughable if it is run off at twice the proper speed,
and if we saw the bewildered women running and drip-
ping at the same time we should understand how they
fit into the whole farcical scheme.

When Shakespeare wrote *The Comedy of Errors* he
was aiming, with great accuracy, at the perennial popular theater. He demanded, therefore, very little of his
audience. He does not expect us to be interested in the
subtleties of character: the figures in this farce are
labeled (as servant, man-about-town, wife or courtesan)
just accurately enough to enable us to tell them apart.
We are not called upon for much sympathy or imagination: in fact we must not try to see through these char-

acters' eyes, or feel what they feel. It would ruin everything to take the wife's troubles, or Dromio's many beatings, at all seriously. All we have to do is grasp the broadly absurd situation, and follow the ingenious fugue of the plot. To get the point, nothing beyond mental alertness of an easy kind is required. The foolishness presented in this play is that of the incredible and arbitrary basic situation, not the ineluctable folly of mankind.

The play belongs in the stream of popular comedy, from Menander to Minsky; but it also shows an intelligence and control, on the part of the author, which is rare in any kind of play. It is much lighter and funnier than *The Two Menaechmuses*. This mastery is revealed, not so much in the language, though that is perfectly adequate to its modest purposes, as in the consistency with which its farcical limitations are accepted, and in the ingenuity of the plot. This plot really is built like the proverbial "Swiss watch": it is as absurdly neat as Leibniz's pre-established harmony. Comedy of this type, or taste—rationalistic, built on a Latin base—was to be more fully explored in the succeeding age of the Enlightenment, in the innumerable comedies which lighted the theaters of Europe from Molière through Mozart. But Shakespeare was developing in a different direction, not toward the univocal perfection of the geometric diagram, but toward the harmonizing of complementary perspectives; not toward further ingenuity, but toward deeper insight.

The Comedy of Errors, like other comedies of that taste, is so clear that it *ought* to be reducible to a formula. Molière's comedies often strike us in the same way. Certainly one can find in them many standard and publicly available devices, whether of plotting, attitude, or conventional characterization. Without that heritage I do not suppose Shakespeare could, at so early an age, have written anything so easy and assured. Yet he uses it for his own purposes, like a good cook who first learns and then forgets the basic recipes, or a dress designer who assumes the clichés of fashion only to go beyond them to something not quite predictable. Only Shakespeare could derive *The Comedy of Errors* from Plautus, and only he could proceed from that simple fun to the enigmatic humor of his maturity.

II

When Shakespeare wrote *Much Ado About Nothing* he had lost none of his skill as a maker of plots; on the contrary, he had attained further mastery in the ten years or more since the writing of *The Comedy of Errors*. There are three main narrative-lines: that of Claudio, Hero, and the wicked Don John; the connected story of Dogberry and the Watch; and the contrasting story of Beatrice and Benedick, all interwoven with clarity and apparent ease. But in this play Shakespeare uses the plot for a further and deeper end. Each of the three narrative-lines has its own humor, and by the interplay of the three a more general vision of man as laughable is suggested: a vision which is at once comic and poetic.

The story of young Claudio and Hero caught in Don John's wicked schemes was Shakespeare's starting point, and the somewhat casual framework of the plot of the whole play. He had read this story in Bandello's version, *Timbreo di Cardona*, the story of a girl unjustly accused of adultery. This tale, though it ends happily, is not very funny in itself, and Shakespeare does not so much avoid its painful and pathetic aspects as absorb them in his more detached comic vision. The scene in the church, when poor Hero is wrongly accused and her father Leonato loudly laments, may be played for a "tragic" effect, but that I think would not be quite right. The audience knows that it is all a mistake, and it is by that time accustomed to smile at Claudio, an absurdly solemn victim of young love's egoism. When he first appears he tries to tell the Duke what the Duke knew already: his all-important love for Hero. He glumly decides that the Duke, wooing Hero in his behalf, has stolen her, and so is wrong again. Beatrice labels him for us: "glum as an orange, and something of that jealous complexion." His false accusation is his third mistake: we must sympathize, but at the same time smile, at this final instance of his foolishness. The whole Claudio-Hero story is comic in itself and in its own way, but to understand what Shakespeare meant by it it is necessary to think of it in relation to the two other stories which unfold in alternation with it.

Dogberry and the Watch are closely connected with the Claudio story, which requires someone to uncover Don John's plot, but Shakespeare developed this element into a farcical sequence with its own tone and interest. At the same time he uses it to lighten the catastrophe at Hero's wedding, and the character of Don John: we cannot take a villain seriously who can be apprehended by Dogberry. Dogberry is not suffering the delusions of young love, like Claudio, but those of vanity and uncontrollable verbosity. His efforts to find his way, with lanterns, through the darkness of the night and the more impenetrable darkness of his wits, forms an ironic parallel to the groping of the young lovers through their mists of feeling. Dogberry also has his version of the underlying mood of the play—that of a leisurely and joyful ease, such as we attribute to Eden or the Golden Age. In Dogberry this infatuated leisureliness, this delusion that nothing terrible can really happen, takes the form of interminable verbalizing while the evil plot hatches and the villains lurk uncaught.

The story of Beatrice and Benedick's self-tormented love affair is entirely Shakespeare's creation. He seems to have felt the need of that pair's intelligence and agility to ventilate Claudio and Hero. We should tire quickly of Claudio's total submersion in love if Benedick were not there, pretending to be too intelligent for that. Hero, who can only sigh and blush, would be too soggy without Beatrice, who can only make sharp remarks, pull pigtails, and stick her tongue out at the boys. But the two contrasting stories together suggest a vision of early infatuation—provided we don't take Shakespeare's characters more seriously than he intended—which is both deeper and more comic than the victims themselves can know.

Beatrice and Benedick are notoriously hard to act on the modern stage, especially in the first two acts, where they indulge in so many quibbles and conceits in the taste of their times. There is no use trying to make the verbal jokes funny; but I am not sure that Shakespeare himself took them seriously as jokes. I once had the pleasure of seeing John Gielgud and Pamela Brown act several of the Beatrice-Benedick scenes. They "threw away" the words, or even, at moments, made fun of their far-fetched elaboration, and by this means focused their audience's attention on the noble, silly, intelligent and bewildered *relation* of the two—a relation as agile, musical, and deeply comic as that of Congreve's reluctant lovers, Mirabel and Millamant. I feel sure that this approach to the play is right: its surfaces, its literal words, characters and events, are not to be taken seriously: the point is in the music of unseen motivation, in the fact that it *is* unseen by the characters themselves—and that all the fun and folly plays against a background of mystery.

The main Claudio-Hero-Don John intrigue is also not to be taken too seriously, as though it were the point of the play: Shakespeare gets it under way casually, after the underlying mood of the play as a whole, and its "action" of elaborate play, or leisurely enjoyment, has been firmly established. The opening scene, in which Leonato's household prepares to celebrate the return of the Duke, Benedick and Claudio from their comic-opera war, tells us what the play is really about: it is a festive occasion, a celebration of a certain evanescent but recurrent human experience. The experience is real in its way, all may recognize it, but under its spell everything the characters do is much ado about nothing. The progress of the underlying action of the play as a whole is therefore marked by a series of somewhat dreamy and deluded festive occasions. The first of these is Leonato's masked ball, in Act II, a visible and musical image of the action. Then comes Dogberry's nocturnal and incomprehensible charge to the Watch: a farcical version of the theme. The fourth act consists chiefly of the marriage which turns out to be no marriage at all, but a bad dream. In the fifth act there is Claudio's funeral tribute to Hero, by night, at her supposed tomb; but this is a funeral which is no funeral, corresponding to the marriage which was no marriage. After that pathetic and comic expiatory rite, daylight returns, the torches are put out, and we are ready for the real and double marriage, in daylight, with the ladies unmasked at last, which ends the play in dance and song.

We are just beginning to understand the technical value of the "ceremonious occasion" as an element of plot, though it has been used in countless ways from Aristophanes to Henry James. When people assemble for a ceremonious occasion (whether it be the festival of Dionysos or one of James's thorny tea parties) they must abate, or conceal, their purely individual purposes, and recognize the common concern which brings them together. A dramatist may use the festive occasion, therefore, to shift his audience's attention from the detail of the literal intrigue to some general plight which all more or less unwittingly share. All are social and political animals; all must suffer spring, mating, and death. Ceremonious occasions are especially useful to dramatists who are seeking poetry, which, as Aristotle remarked, is concerned with something more general than the particular facts, the unique events, of human life. The point—the comic point—of *Much Ado*—is poetic in that sense, and hence it is the festive ensemble scenes which most clearly adumbrate the basic vision of the play. In this respect the plot of *Much Ado* contrasts sharply with that of *The Comedy of Errors*. The point of that play lies precisely in the unique situation of mistaken identity, and in the strings of absurd events which quickly follow from it. An "occasion" of any kind would break the tight concatenation of *contretemps;* and that Shakespeare is careful to avoid doing until he is ready to end the whole play.

One might say that *Much Ado* presents a comic vision of mankind which is also poetic, while the purpose of *The Comedy of Errors* is closer to that of the professional vaudevillian, who gauges his success by clocking the laughs: the provoking of thoughtless mirth, an almost reflex response. The difference between the two plays is clearest, perhaps, when one reflects that both are concerned with mistaken identity, but in *The Comedy of Errors* the mistake is simply a mistake in fact, while in *Much Ado* it is a failure of insight, or rather many failures of different kinds by the different characters.

Shakespeare accomplishes the *dénouement* of *The Comedy of Errors* in one swift scene. It is not difficult to correct an error in fact: it may be done instantly by providing the right fact: and as soon as both pairs of twins are on stage together, the error is gone. But correcting a failure of insight is a most delicate and mysterious process, which Shakespeare suggests, in *Much Ado,* in countless ways: through the symbolism of masks, night, and verbal ambiguities, and in peripeteias of his three variously comic subplots.

The farcical efforts of Dogberry and Verges never deviate into enlightenment. They learn as little as the characters in *The Comedy of Errors:* but, like them, they do stumble eventually upon the right fact: they manage to apprehend the villains and convey that fact to Leonato.

Claudio, with his dark fumes of love, has a long way

to go before he can see anything real. After his false wedding Shakespeare puts him through a false and painful challenge from his best friend, Benedick, and then the mocking (but touching) mummery of his visit to Hero's empty tomb. Even then the audience learns more from Claudio's masquerade-like progress through the maze than he does himself.

Beatrice and Benedick come the closest, of all the characters, to grasping the whole scope of the comic vision which the play slowly unfolds. But even after their friends have tried to kid them out of their frightened vanity during the first three acts, it takes most of the fourth and fifth acts, where all the painful things occur, to bring them to conscious acceptance of their absurd selves, each other, and their love. It is the fiasco of Claudio's first attempt at marriage which marks the crucial turn in their relationship:

Benedick: Lady Beatrice, have you wept all this while?
Beatrice: Yea, and I will weep a while longer.

and a little later:

Benedick: I do love nothing in the world so well as you. Is not that strange?
Beatrice: As strange as the thing I know not. It were as possible for me to say I love nothing so well as you; but believe me not; and yet I lie not; I confess nothing. . . .

In this exchange the love-warmed final scene of the play is foreshadowed, but the misfortunes of Claudio and Hero, which here bring Beatrice and Benedick near together, immediately carry them apart again. Benedick has to challenge Claudio, and that boy's delusions have to be repented and dispelled, before Beatrice and Benedick can trust their intuition of love, or accept it fully and in good conscience. I do not attempt to follow the subtle shifts in their relationship which Shakespeare suggests,

in a few quick, sure strokes, during the fifth act. But it is
Beatrice and Benedick who dominate the final scene:

Benedick: Soft and fair, Friar. Which is Beatrice?

Bea. (unmasking): I answer to that name. What is your
will?

Ben.: Do not you love me?

Bea.: Why no, no more than reason.

Ben.: Why then, your uncle and the Prince and Claudio
have been deceived; they swore you did.

Bea.: Do not you love me?

Ben.: Troth no, no more than reason.

Bea.: Why then my cousin, Margaret, and Ursula are
much deceived, for they did swear you did.

(Claudio and Hero produce love letters from Benedick
and Beatrice to each other)

Ben.: A miracle! here's our own hands against our
hearts. Come, I will have thee; but, by this light,
I take thee for pity.

Bea.: I would not deny you, but by this good day I
yield upon great persuasion, and partly to save
your life, for I was told you were in a consump-
tion.

Ben.: Peace; I will stop your mouth.

In this scene the main contrasting themes of the play
are brought together, and very lightly and quickly resolved: marriage true and false, masking and unmasking,
the delusion and truth of youthful love. The harmonies
may all be heard in Beatrice's and Benedick's words. The
exchange is in prose, but (like the prose of Leonato's
masked ball) it has a rhythm and a varied symmetry
suggesting the formality of a dance figure. The key
words—love, reason, day, light, pity, peace—make music
both for the ear and for the understanding as they echo
back and forth, deepening in meaning with each new
context. The effect of the scene as a whole is epitomized
in Beatrice's and Benedick's heavenly double-take: their

foolish idiosyncrasy is clear, but some joyful flood of acceptance and understanding frees them, for the moment, and lifts them beyond it. Is this effect "comic"? I do not know; I think it is intended to bring a smile, not for the windup of this little plot, but for the precarious human condition.

When one reads *Much Ado* in the security of one's own room, indulging in daydreams of an ideal performance, it is possible to forget the practical and critical problems which surround the question of the play's viability in our time. But it must be admitted that high school productions are likely to be terribly embarrassing, and I do not even like to think of the play's pathetic vulnerability on Times Square. The play demands much from its performers, almost as much as Chekhov does. It demands a great deal from its audience: a leisurely and contemplative detachment which seems too costly in our hustled age. Perhaps Shakespeare should be blamed for all this: if *Much Ado* does not easily convince us on the contemporary stage, perhaps we should conclude, as Eliot once concluded of *Hamlet,* that it is an artistic failure. But on that principle we should have to rule out a great deal of Shakespeare. It was his habit, not only in *Hamlet* and *Much Ado,* but in many other plays, to indicate, rather than explicitly to present, his central theme; and to leave it to his performers and his audience to find it behind the varied episodes, characters, and modes of language which are literally presented. Everything which Shakespeare meant by *The Comedy of Errors* is immediately perceptible; the comic vision of *Much Ado* will only appear, like the faces which Dante saw in the milky substance of the moon, slowly, and as we learn to trust the fact that it is really there.

PART III

Critical Attitudes

"Myth" and the Literary Scruple

"MYTH" is one of those words which it has become almost impossible to use without apologetic quotation marks. Ill-defined for centuries, it is now used in many senses and for many purposes: to mean nonsense or willful obscurantism in some contexts, the deepest wisdom of man in others. One would like to be able to banish it to that pale Hades where "irony" and "ambiguity" have their impotent but pretentious afterlife. But unfortunately the student of literature cannot get along without "myth." It is too evident that poetry, to say nothing of religion, philosophy and history, are akin to mythopoeia. Drama, the lyric and fiction live symbiotically with myths, nourished by them, and nourishing their flickering lives. Some of the inventions of poets—Kafka's *Metamorphosis*, Plato's tale of the charioteer with his white and his black horse—are modeled on myth. Some poetic works which we like—*Moby Dick*, Lorca's plays—have what we are pleased to call a "mythic" quality. Writers of all kinds use inherited myths in their own work. The student of literature cannot avoid talking about myth; but how can he use the protean word with any decent rigor?

It was the early romantic poets and philosophers who started our modern cult of myth. They sought in it some alternative to the narrow categories of modern rationalism, some defense of humane letters in a world created by applied science; often they felt it would replace formal religion. But in our time scientists and pseudo-scientists of every description—psychologists of several persuasions; archeologists, linguists, assorted varieties of anthropologists and sociologists—pronounce upon myth with an imposing air of authority. And specialists in various fields have filled our books and our museums with countless mythic tales and mythic figures, not only from our own tradition but from every corner of the human time and space. In this welter of facts and theories the student of literature is in danger of losing his bearings altogether. For he cannot simply disregard the labors of countless savants on myth; he must use them for his own purposes when they strike him as illuminating. On the other hand, he lacks the knowledge and the training to join the debates of specialists on their own terms. What he needs, I think, is a renewed sense of his own stake in myth, plus a firmer reliance on the evidences in literature and on the methods and the criteria of literary analysis. For the point at which myth concerns the student of literature is the point at which it is brought to life again in poetry, drama or fiction.

From this point of view it is evident that it is not realistic to talk about myth-in-general, as though we had a generally agreed upon definition which would apply to all the instances of myth in art and letters. And if one makes the all-important distinction between the second-hand, merely reported or summarized, mythic tale, as we find it in Bulfinch or *The Hero with a Thousand Faces,* and the mythic tale as it actually lives in poetry or drama, it appears that we lack an unmistakable example of even *one* myth. For the myth of Oedipus is one thing in *Oedipus Rex*, and something quite different in the dramas of Seneca or Dryden. Giraudoux, clearly recognizing this point, called his play *Amphytrion 38.* One of the most striking properties of myths is that they generate new forms (like the differing children of one parent) in the imaginations of those who try to grasp them. Until some imagination, that of a poet or only a reader or auditor, is thus fecundated by a myth, the myth would seem to exist only potentially. And if we cannot lay hands on even one myth prior to its imaginative embodiments, how can we hope to pin down myth-in-general in *it*self?

We must, I think, adopt an extremely ascetic regimen in our dealings with myth. We must abandon hope of reaching any very plausible generalizations, and pay close attention to some of the many ways in which myths actually live in our literature. Of course the evidence, even when thus arbitrarily reduced, is almost endless, and very diverse. How can we rule out any of the living works which the narrative in the Christian Creed at one extreme, the lightest tale of Ovid at the other have generated in the imaginations of artists in thousands of years? All one could hope to do is to choose rather haphazardly a few examples, as illustrations of what a literary approach to myth might be.

Let us begin with a rough preliminary classification of the kinds of myths to be found in literature. The classification I wish to propose is taken from Malinowski's study of the Trobriand Islanders. He found three types of myth in that culture: Legends, which he defined as stories about the past which were believed to be true of the past, and which served to give the Islanders some significant conception of their history; Folk or Fairy Tales, told only for fun, without reference to truth, on occasions when the tribe was gathered simply for entertainment; and Religious Myths, which represented basic elements in the creed, the morals, and the social structure of that people. Malinowski based this classification on his observations of the Trobrianders, but it looks as though he had understood them by analogy with our own culture, for we can recognize the three types (or the three attitudes to myth) in our art and literature. Some scientific anthropologists mistrust Malinowski pre-

cisely because he feels the kinship between the Trobrianders and us; but for me his value lies in his sympathy and his sense of the humane analogies between
cultures. Let us claim him for the Humanities, and see
how his classification may help us to understand our own
heritage.

I think we should have to go back to Dante's Chris-
tianized Vergilian Legend of Rome to find a fully developed Historic Legend in Malinowski's sense. But the
Fairy Tales, Little Red Riding Hood, the innumerable
Greek tales of Arcady, of nymphs and shepherds,
charming stories whose truth we never enquire into, have
been common since the early Renaissance. Readers of
Professor Douglas Bush's studies of literary myths will
think of countless examples. It is easy to see why the
fairy tale conception of myth is quite at home in times
of the most intransigent rationalism. If the myth makes
no claim to truth in itself, but at most serves as pleasing
illustration of some moral or political concept, we may
enjoy it with a clear conscience. But the romantic and
post-romantic cult of myth is not content with these neoclassic attitudes. It seeks the religious myth, or tries to
attribute metaphysical meaning to the myths it invokes.
Most of the contemporary debates about myth assume
this religious intention on the part of the lovers of myth,
and so we have many interesting attempts (like Wheel-
wright's in *The Burning Fountain* or Campbell's in *The
Hero with a Thousand Faces*) to defend myth as a mode
of knowing.

But the most natural view of myth in the modern
world (by which I mean our tradition since Dante defined the "allegory of poets") has been the fairy tale conception. And in the hands of Paul Valéry this way with
myth has turned out to have new vitality. No one could
accuse Valéry of underestimating reason, the usual com-
plaint of users of myths in our time. He is the champion
of *l'intelligence*, the emancipated but scrupulous mind,
reason at its most ambitious and austere: the ultimate

reliance of modernists, from Socrates through Da Vinci to Valéry himself. And at the same time he is the high priest of pure poetry, "the representative poet of the first half of the Twentieth Century," as Eliot called him. His poetry should therefore be a crucial instance of the life of myth in literature.

The first line of his *Fragments du Narcisse* announces the theme of that poem:

> *Que tu brilles enfin, terme pur de ma course!*

We are to imagine Narcissus bending over the pool, addressing his own shining reflection as the pure goal, now recognized at last, of his life's course. Then come the beautiful music and the Arcadian imagery of the *Fragments:* the reeds, the water, the quiet evening, the echoes and reflections which echo and reflect the inward focus of thought and desire. The poem has the magic suggestiveness, or call it the abstract allusiveness, of the finest *symboliste* achievements, and I do not therefore attempt to analyze it in detail. Suffice it to say that as we let the poem sink in we come to see that the first line is to be understood in more senses than one. It is not only Narcissus' address to his reflection, it is the poet's address to Narcissus, who illustrates the paradoxical goal of pure reason and also of pure poetry. Thus it is also the poet's invocation of his own spirit at that creative center of life where thought and poetic intuition both have their source. When the life of reason attains its highest abstraction its pleasure lies in contemplating itself in the act of contemplation. And when poetry is pure enough—approaching the abstractness of music, freeing itself from all attachment, whether to persons, things, or transcendent moral or religious goals —it becomes its own object. The best poems in Valéry's *symboliste* tradition are based on the sad delectation of poetry's self-love.

It is easy to see why Narcissus is addressed by Valéry as the very image of his own goal. Narcissus aptly represents Valéry's lifelong study: the mind's creative or formative power when it turns inward in search of itself. The perversity of the mythic figure, the futility of introversion even when most subtle, is part of the poet's gloomy meaning. And yet the question of the reality of Narcissus himself never arises. The poet is not interested in exploring the mythic narrative itself. He does not present the thwarted nymphs who beseech Narcissus in vain (except in Narcissus' vague fear of their interruption) nor the fight, nor the transformation of Narcissus himself into that pretty specimen of vegetable life, the narcissus flower, which seems so suggestive in any realistic reading of the story. The figure of Narcissus is perhaps the "inspiration" of the poem, as a metaphor or even a word may be; but its value remains strictly poetic. In all of this Valéry accepts the fairy tale notion of myth, handling it lightly, almost playfully, as though for entertainment only. His use of his myth is basically a more sophisticated version of the neoclassic convention: as a language, closely analogous to the endlessly worked-over but still iridescent words of French. Hence the deflated exactitude of the Valérian taste, the crystalline hardness one feels beneath the shimmer of his effects.

Valéry as *symboliste* represents a culmination of the romantic movement, its "classic" moment of complete self-awareness, as he himself would put it. He is concerned with the unique essence of poetry and its absolute independence; in his hands myth serves poetry, not vice versa. Though he is the heir of the romantic poets he does not have a trace of their religious attitude to Myth. This is Malinowski's description of the Religious Myth—the "myth proper" as he calls it—among the Trobrianders:

A special class of stories, regarded as sacred, embodied in ritual, morals and social organization. . . . These stories live not by idle interest . . . but are to the natives a statement of a primeval, greater and more relevant reality, by which the present life, fates and activities of mankind are determined, the knowledge of which supplies man with the motive for ritual and moral actions, as well as with indications how to perform them.

Valéry could accept none of this without betraying his faith in the independent formative power of the mind. But Malinowski's description applies by analogy to the narrative in the Christian Creed, the basis of European social and cultural order, and of much of European art, for a thousand years. And it applies also to what romantic poets seek vaguely, and more or less in vain, in the myths which they religiously invoke.

Wagner's *Tristan und Isolde* is the most perfect example I know of the romantic-religious cult of myth. Thus Wagner opposes to Valéry's rationalist tradition, in which the mythic tales are told for fun or half-playfully allegorized, the Tristan narrative, in which he finds a "primeval, greater and more relevant reality" than that of reason and common sense. Valéry in *Narcisse* appeals to the individual intellect and its strictly poetic sensibility, but Wagner, basing all on the power of his music, reaches for a primitive, unindividualized mode of awareness in his hypnotized and moblike audience. Valéry does not take the Narcissus story seriously except as metaphor or illustration, but Wagner makes the course of the Tristan narrative the very form, or "soul," of the opera. Each crucial episode: the drinking of the love potion, the single night of love, the final *Liebestod*: has a ritual significance which perhaps reflects (as De Rougemont suggests) the rites of the half-forgotten cult of the Cathari. Valéry expects no result from his poem but the refined pleasures of the mind and the sensibility, but Wagner wants to effect an initiation or change of heart, and the final love-death seems to demand a momentary faith, at least, in a greater, unseen reality. We know that there is, in fact, a Wagnerian cult, which helped to nourish Hitler's attempt to create a German

Volk by magic. One may even see in Schopenhauer, in Nietzsche's *Birth of Tragedy,* and in Freud, with his death-wish and his boundless libido, a kind of theology for the gloomy-religious action of *Tristan.*

Wagner's treatment of the Tristan myth fulfills the requirements of Malinowski's definition of the religious myth. It also agrees with what Maritain has to say of "metaphysical myths" in his *Creative Intuition:* "The metaphysical myths are the organic signs and symbols of some faith actually lived. . . . They are forms through which a conviction of the entire soul nourishes and quickens from within the very power of creative imagination. Such myths have no force except through the faith man has in them." Wagner must, I think, have worked upon *Tristan* with the faith which Maritain describes, for the creative power of the opera is unmistakable. But unfortunately a faith may be desperate and deluded when one sees in "myth a source of higher teaching and ultraspiritual insights, converting it into a magic mirror that reflects the heart's desire," as Philip Rahv says of the romantic cult of myth. Wagner's religious acceptance of the Tristan myth is possible only at too great an expense: the rejection of the contemporary world along with all the achievements of reason, from morality to science. Those who see in the cult of myth only willful obscurantism would find much in Wagner to support their thesis. And such reflections as these must throw some doubt on the faith which Wagner himself had in the "greater and more relevant reality" symbolized by *Tristan;* we know that he changed his mind about it later in his life.

The fact is that we are here in that dim and treacherous realm between firm religious belief on one side and make-believe on the other. Belief and make-believe have similar fertilizing effects upon human creativity. An actor must make-believe his role very deeply and with full concentration if he is to give more than a superficial performance, yet we do not attribute religious faith to him, even when we in the audience "believe" in the character he is presenting. And in our time we are more at home with make-believe than we are with belief—or perhaps we have simply lost the sense of the distinction. Even the truths of science begin to look like partial metaphors: necessary (though sometimes contradictory) hypotheses, which guide and nourish the scientific imagination for a time, not adequate and final truth. Thus the whole problem of the religious myth is on the edge of an even darker mystery: that of the nature, even the possibility, of real faith in our time.

That is one important reason why, in our attempt to collect the crucial evidences of poetry as it reincarnates myths, we must at this point remember Dante. For in the *Divine Comedy* we unmistakably encounter the solidity of real belief. That poem, based on the Christian Creed, celebrates the faith and the moral, philosophic, and liturgical order which regulated Europe from the Dark Ages to the threshold of modern times: that "primeval, greater and more relevant reality" which Malinowski says the religious myth, the "myth proper," is supposed to embody. The *Divine Comedy* would, for this reason alone, be required reading for the study of the life of myth in poetry.

Moreover the *Divine Comedy* contains all the kinds of myth, and all the attitudes to myth, which Malinowski describes, all in significant relation to each other and to the enlightened Reason of Dante's time. Thus Malinowski's "historic legend" is built into the framework of the poem: Vergil's legendary interpretation of Rome, which Dante combines with the historic drama of the Old Testament and places in the perspective of the Incarnation, wherein both the Hebrew and the pagan traditions are fulfilled. This historical legend serves exactly the purpose Malinowski describes: based on the known facts of the past, which are accepted as true of the past, it gives Dante's generation its bearings in the historic sequence. What Malinowski calls fairy tales—the loot of

Ovid and Lucan, more obscure tales from Arabic or
Celtic sources—are alive again in every part of the
Comedy. Dante takes them in a spirit akin to Valéry's:
"my not-false errors" he calls them, when they inspire
his imagination on the purgatorial stair. They provide
much of the great poem's sensuous movement and
variety; and when we look more closely we see that each
has also its tropological meaning: they are visionary embodiments of the momentary experiences of the pilgrim
spirit as the moral life unfolds. The ultimate meaning of
the moral life, like that of the life of the race in history,
is seen in the Incarnation and Sacrifice of Christ. It is
that narrative, of course, which commands Dante's real
belief and provides (quite apart from the question of
our belief) the very pattern of the religious myth.

A real study of Dante's masterful way with his vast
heritage of myths would require not minutes but years;
and it would require a combination of erudition and tact
which is not available. But one may get some slight
sense of his virtuosity from almost any detail of the
poem. Consider, for instance, what he does with the
Siren in the dream which forms the opening sequence
of *Purgatorio* XIX:

> Nell'ora che non può il calor diurno
>   intiepidar più il freddo della luna,
>   vinto da terra o talor da Saturno;
> quando i geomanti lor maggior fortuna
>   veggiono in oriente, inanzi all'alba,
>   surger per via che poco le sta bruna:
> mi venne in sogno una femmina balba,
>   negli occhi guercia e sopra i piè distorta,
>   con le man monche, e di colore scialba.
> Io la mirava; e come il sol conforta
>   le fredde membra che la notte aggrava,
>   così lo sguardo mio le facea scorta
> la lingua, e poscia tutta la drizzava
>   in poco d'ora, e lo smarrito volto,

come amor vuol, così le colorava.
Poi ch'ell'avea il parlar così disciolto,
    cominciava a cantar sì che con pena
    da lei avrei mio intento rivolto.
"Io son," cantava, "io son dolce Sirena,
    che i marinari in mezzo mar dismago:
    tanto son di piacere a sentir piena.
"Io volsi Ulisse del suo cammin vago
    col canto mio; e qual meco si ausa
    rado sen parte, sì tutto l'appago."
Ancor non era sua bocca richiusa,
    quando una donna apparve santa e presta
    lunghesso me per far colei confusa.
"O Virgilio, o Virgilio, chi è questa?"
    fieramente diceva; ed ei venia
    con gli occhi fitti pure in quella onesta.
L'altra prendeva, e dinanzi l'apria
    fendendo i drappi, e mostravami il ventre;
    quel mi svegliò col puzzo che n'uscia.

(At the hour when the heat of the day can no longer
warm the cold of the moon, being overcome by earth or
perhaps by Saturn;

When the geomancers see their *fortuna major* in the east,
just before dawn, rising along a path which will not be
dark for long:

There came to me in dream a stuttering woman, squint-
eyed, twisted on her feet, with stunted hands, yellow in
color.

I gazed upon her, and as the sun comforts cold limbs
which night weighs down, so my gaze made ready

Her tongue, and then in a short time set her all straight,
and her pale face, just as love wills, it colored.

As soon as her speech was loosened she began to sing, so
that with difficulty I should have turned my attention
from her.

"I am," she sang, "I am that sweet Siren who bemuses
sailors in the midst of the sea, so full I am of pleasure
for them to feel.

"I turned Ulysses from his wandering way to this my song; whoever risks himself with me rarely departs, I satiate him so fully."

Her mouth was hardly closed when there appeared beside me a woman, alert and holy, to make that one confused.

"O Vergil, Vergil, who is this?" she was saying proudly, and he was coming, with his eyes fixed only on that honest one.

He seized the other and opened her in front, ripping the clothes, and showed me the belly, which waked me with the stench that issued from it.) *

Dante's treatment of the Siren in this passage is similar in several ways to Valéry's treatment of Narcissus: it is an example of Dante's "allegory of poets." Thus, like Valéry, he is more interested in the mythic figure than in her whole traditional story, and he uses her to get the sensuous immediacy and the subtle complexity of poetry. But she seems to have more reality than Valéry's conventional figure: if not a metaphysical entity in her own right, she is at least an ineluctable trope, the embodiment of one eternally-recurrent human experience. That is because the Siren has her place in a vaster vision which includes the perspectives of ethics and faith. Valéry's Narcissus, on the other hand, is presented as "pure" poetry.

Dante establishes the being and the meanings of his Siren by means of the context in which she appears: a certain point in the Pilgrim's spiritual growth, at a certain place on the Mountain, and toward the end of the second night of the purgatorial journey. By showing us the psyche in whose imagination the Siren appears, Dante includes several dimensions of mythopoeia which Valéry omits. We *see* the dreamer see his mythic enchantress, an image which at first says nothing to him. We then see him "believe" the image, and focus his at-

* *The Purgatoria of Dante Alishieri*, Temple Classics Edition, London.

tention and his unsatisfied desire upon it. Under that
warmth and light the ancient myth, "colored as love
wills," reveals some of the meanings she had held only
potentially: in short, she is "brought to life." But the
night in which she appears also helps us to understand
her. In all three nights of the purgatorial journey the
Pilgrim can rely neither upon his direct perception of
the world, his moral will, or his reason. In the solitude
and passivity of sleep he knows the call of many forms
of love, including that irrational brute weight of desire
which pulls, like gravitation, toward the bottom of the
universe. In this passage the nocturnal chill that weighs
limbs down presents this pull: the occasion for the
Siren's appearance. The direction of love's movement
thus indicated (night against reason and the day, the
ambiguity of love and death) reminds one strongly of
the motivation and the nocturnal imagery of *Tristan*.
Dante may have seen at this point the object of Wagner's desperate faith.

But this is the *second* night of the purgatorial journey,
and the Pilgrim has by this time acquired a certain moral
awareness. After the Siren is warmed into beauty and
song, at the very moment of pleasurable yielding, Vergil
appears by that Grace which hovers over this region,
and reveals the Siren's deathly aspect once more. Vergil
represents reason and the accumulated wisdom of experience in the real world, and by this time his voice
and presence are in a sense *within* the Pilgrim's spirit.
In the dream he plays a role like that of the orthodox
Freudian "superego," representative of moral truth. At
this point in his development the Pilgrim (and the
reader) can understand the mythic Siren from a moral
point of view, and that suffices for escape.

But because of the sturdy realism which underlies the
whole conception of the *Divine Comedy* the Siren, for
all her moral meaning, is not reduced to the status of a
moral allegory only. She retains some sort of being in
her own right; she does not forfeit her status as one of

the amoral figures of myth, and that is characteristic of Dante's way with myths. Their visionary being is established first, their possible philosophical meaning for the Pilgrim, second; and when they disappear we do not feel that they have been rationalized out of all existence. The Siren first looks strange and evil, then she appears as infinitely attractive, then as dismaying and disgusting, but in all of these metamorphoses we never lose the sense that she was somehow *there;* and her power and mystery remain when we leave her.

If Dante can handle the figures of myth with such subtle and flexible realism—that is, with respect both for the reality of the imagination in which they appear, and for the different reality of the figures themselves—it is because he understands them, not in conceptual terms, but by analogy with the Incarnation. The process whereby a myth is brought to life in a human imagination corresponds to that by which Christ lives again in the spirits of the faithful, through belief, concentration, love, and an imitative movement of spirit. The mythic forms which tempt the human spirit may in Dante's scheme be childish or deceptive. But their meaning for us and the process whereby we reincarnate them in our own beings are to be understood by analogy with the human figure, and the imitation, of Christ. Even Hell, where Dante endows so many evil forms with his own life and love, was made by Divine Power, Highest Wisdom and Primal Love. It is because Dante believes so completely in the reality of this basic Analogue that he can both share in the lives of many kinds of myths, and yet also pass beyond them, to consider their meaning in other terms and in relation to each other. His belief in the "primeval, greater and more relevant reality" of the Christian Narrative gives him a key to the heritage of myth, makes him a master (probably *the* master) of the mythic modes of understanding.

The view of the world which Dante inherited, formed by the converging and agelong labors of Hebrew and

Greek, has dissolved long since. His *modus vivendi* between Reason and Mythopoeia is no longer accessible to us. But if we are to consider the life of myth in the poetry of our tradition, I do not see how we can continue to neglect the vast lore in the *Divine Comedy*.

One can sympathize with those numerous writers who use "myth" to mean only wishful thinking or Machiavellian obscurantism. It would be nice to get rid of the term and its puzzles so simply. But that recourse is not available to those who stubbornly continue to be interested in poetry, or indeed in any form of the humanities. We cannot get rid of "myth," but we can beware of it. We can remember some of the countless ways in which myths live in our literature from Homer to Faulkner. And we can study some of the forms this life takes with the respect for the unique individuality of play or poem which the masters of literature have taught us.

The Golden Bowl Revisited

SINCE 1933, when I first attempted a reading of *The Golden Bowl*, much illuminating work has been done on that novel and on James in general. We have had the background studies of Matthiessen and Edel, for example, and critical comments by many acute students, including Dupee, Spender, Edmund Wilson, F. R. Leavis, and most recently R. P. Blackmur, in his introduction to the new edition of the novel. The effect of these studies has been to emphasize again the importance of *The Golden Bowl* in the Jamesian canon, but not to produce general agreement on its value and meaning. Mr. Leavis thinks it marks the decay of James's art, while Mr. Blackmur presents it as one of his greatest and most poetic achievements.

Moreover, in 1946 Mr. Quentin Anderson published an essay in *The Kenyon Review* entitled "Henry James and the New Jerusalem," which shows James in a totally new light. He demonstrated the great influence of Henry senior's philosophy upon his son's art, especially that of *The Ambassadors, The Wings of the Dove,* and *The Golden Bowl*. These three novels, he explained, constitute an elaborate allegory based upon his father's version of Swedenborg's philosophy. Mr. Anderson's essay was convincing to me, and now he has expanded it to the length of a book, and he has been kind enough to allow me to read it in manuscript. The longer study is far more detailed, and even more persuasive, than the essay. I think that Mr. Anderson's claim for his discovery is not excessive, that it "requires a recasting of our views, not simply of James, but also of his affiliations with the writers of his time and of our own"—and, I should like to add, writers long before his time: Vergil, Dante, the late Shakespeare, who wrote allegories of Western history and of the human spirit's progress akin to that of Swedenborg and Henry James the elder. This unfamiliar view of James and his place in the world of letters has not yet been digested, though Mr. Leavis has recognized it and commented upon it briefly.

Of course a recasting of our view of James and his place in the tradition is not a job to be got out of the way in a short paper. But I should like to raise some of the questions that suggest themselves about *The Golden Bowl*, and, more particularly, the question of the nature of the allegorical method of this novel. What is the relation between the novel we know, the novel I thought I had read twenty years ago, and the minutely worked-out allegorical meaning which Mr. Anderson has demonstrated?

The allegorical meaning of the late trilogy is simply the elder James's religious-historical philosophy. *"The Ambassadors, The Wings of the Dove,* and *The Golden Bowl,"* Mr. Anderson writes, "comprise a spiritual cosmology which may be called the divine novel. They deal respectively with the three principal churches of our history, the Jewish, the Christian, and the New Church." According to the elder James, following Swedenborg, the Jewish Church was the church of moral righteousness and external, institutionalized Law. The conception is like St. Paul's interpretation of Mosaic Law: the Law convicts us of sin, and offers the notion of righteousness as literal obedience. Henry James the elder encountered that kind of righteousness at the Princeton Theological Seminary when he studied there as a young man. By "the Jewish Church" he means not only Old Testament legalism, but any authoritarian institution: Roman Law, the Christian churches, the forms of society. He thought this "church" evil because it encouraged the worship of the moral will and the aggrandizement of the ego. The Christian Church corrects this moralism by substituting understanding for law, and love for the moral will. This also suggests St. Paul. Christ demonstrated the possibility of uniting man and God, healing the rift between sin and the Law by a spontaneous movement of love. But for James the elder, and Swedenborg, the Christian revelation availed for individuals only: insofar as the Christian Church is institutionalized and legalized it becomes the Jewish Church all over again. The New Church announced by Swedenborg will arrive when mankind as a whole is redeemed. There will be no laws, then; no moral righteousness, and no institutions. God will be within all the free and loving individuals who compose that Golden Saeculum. It is a Utopian vision, akin to many hopeful creeds which moved men in the nineteenth century, especially in America. It is a secular and anthropocentric version of the traditional notion of Eden regained—Dante's Paradiso Terrestre—where (or when) freedom and obedience, man, nature, and God, are one in innocence.

The Ambassadors, the first novel in James's trilogy, deals with the Jewish Church. In that novel, Mr. Anderson explains, "the pinched and wintry Congregationalism of New England stands for Old Testament righteousness. Its chief representative, Lambert Strether, comes not too late but too soon to live." Strether, in middle age, is sent from Massachusetts to Paris to save his friend's son from that wicked city. Instead of rescuing Chad, he is convinced that he himself, with his narrow code of righteousness, has missed life. *"The Wings of the Dove,"* Mr. Anderson continues, "logically follows an account of the failure of the Law or Jewish Church to cope with evil, since it is a poem in which Densher is constrained

178

to accept divine love." In that novel Milly Theale, the American heiress of extraordinary purity and innocence, visits London, where the social forms and appearances embody the evil of human presumption, accepts that burden of evil, and reveals divine love to Densher, who had inhabited his London Hell without light. Like Dante's Beatrice, she plays a role in Densher's life analogous to that of Christ; and (again like Beatrice) she dies, and exercises her loving constraint from beyond the grave. *The Wings of the Dove* thus represents the elder James's "Christian Church," a revelation without laws or institutions. "*The Golden Bowl*," Mr. Anderson goes on, "is a logical sequel to *The Wings of the Dove*, since it deals with the coming of the divine-natural humanity (the New Church)—or (in other words) the 'marriage' of the infinite and the finite." In *The Golden Bowl* Maggie Verver corresponds to Milly Theale. She also is an American heiress of divine innocence, and she too saves her beloved, Prince Amerigo, from the wicked glories of the Old World. But she does not die; on the contrary, she lives to make good her marriage to Amerigo, and to produce with him a son, the Principino, who represents the divine-natural man, the redeemed humanity of the New Church. *The Golden Bowl* is thus the culmination and resolution of that dramatic theme which engaged James all his life—the many-sided conflict between American innocence and European experience. Maggie is that Jamesian American pilgrim who most unmistakably reaches the end of her journey. She is not lost or thwarted; she does not die; she learns how to master the evil which goes with the riches of European experience without losing her own *Édénique* inspiration, her innocent version of love.

I cannot attempt to do justice to Mr. Anderson's very detailed demonstration of the allegory in *The Golden Bowl*. I must refer the reader to his work, and in the meantime merely suggest its main outlines.

Every character in the novel represents an element

in the elder James's philosophy, and the plot is based upon his Swedenborgian scenario of Western history and of the individual's spiritual growth. Thus Adam Verver, Maggie's fabulously rich father, represents divine wisdom and its power. Prince Amerigo, an Italian with the Roman Empire and the Roman Church in his history, represents natural man: he is fully equipped with the lusts of the flesh and the spirit, subject to the uncandid laws of the institutionalized "church," yet still capable of being saved if divine love is revealed to him. Maggie represents this divine love. Charlotte Stant, with her beauty, her sophistication, and her total blindness to divine love, represents all that the Prince naturally lusts after—all that the ancient institutions of Europe sustain. Fanny Assingham, a London hostess who owes her position to shrewdness rather than wealth, represents these ancient social forms, the "Jewish Church" in the elder James's terminology. Her lewd name shows what Henry junior thought of her. She protects Charlotte, who seduces the Prince, by preserving the forms. In the long run Maggie saves the Prince from both women by accepting the evil in which he moves, and showing him divine love. In this she is subtly sustained by her father (divine wisdom), who marries Charlotte and takes her back to America—divine wisdom, inspired by divine love, bringing the unregenerate human ego under control. That leaves the "marriage of the infinite and finite"— divine love and natural man—intact; and the Principino, divine-natural man, as its growing hope.

The Bowl itself is a static and diagrammatic symbol of these relationships. It is made of gilded crystal, a bowl supported by a round foot and a short stem. The foot represents the material root of human life, the stem those rationalized institutions, church, society, forms, appearances, which hold up the human ego: all that the beautiful Charlotte means to the Prince. This Bowl is not only fake, mere gilded crystal, it also has a fatal crack. It represents human life, not as it should be, but

as it is until the New Church comes. The true Bowl of
human life would be upheld by a stem consisting,
not of human institutions and laws, but of divine wisdom; and it would contain, not the gratifications represented by Charlotte, but the divine love represented by
Maggie. The Bowl which is a false simulacrum appears
first when Charlotte wants to give it to Maggie as a
wedding present, but is prevented by the Prince, who
sees the crack. It reappears at the end when Maggie
discovers it by chance, evidence of the Prince's affair with
Charlotte, and Fanny smashes it to preserve appearances. Mr. Anderson has traced the meanings of the
Bowl and its part in the plot in great detail.

I think we must accept Mr. Anderson's thesis, that the
"allegorical meaning" of the novel is the elder James's
theodicy. And yet the novel without the allegory has its
"meaning" too. What is the relation between the two?
Did James himself consider that question when he
worked out the allegory in such detail, yet concealed it
so carefully? Such puzzles must occupy James's critics
for a long time.

Let us forget both the allegory and the novel as we
read it, and consider the bald facts of the story. A very
rich American, Adam Verver, has come to Europe with
his daughter Maggie. He is now one of the world's great
art collectors. He purchases a husband for Maggie,
Amerigo, a wonderful Italian Prince, whom he regards
as the prize *objet d'art* in his collection. Adam himself
then marries Charlotte Stant, a woman of his daughter's
age, on the ground that the Ververs need her beauty and
grand manner to complete their household; Charlotte
is also a very valuable item, a companion-piece to the
Prince. But Charlotte seduces the Prince, for both of
them are terribly bored by their roles as *bibelots* in the
somewhat airless and speechless Verver rooms; and then
of course Maggie feels cheated and helpless. Her father
then applies the cruel torsion of his money-power.
Neither Charlotte nor the Prince can resist that: penni-

less themselves, they require great wealth to live up, not only to the Ververs' requirements, but to their own conceptions of themselves. Adam takes Charlotte back to America, like a handsome panther on a silken rope, and the Prince is restored to Maggie.

In these terms the story is trite, and not very edifying, as Mr. Leavis has pointed out with his usual vigor. He decides that the late James—the James of this trilogy—had "let his moral sense slip into abeyance." He cannot believe that James really knew what he was doing. "That in our feelings about the Ververs there would be any element of distaste, Henry James seems to have had no inkling," says Mr. Leavis, and he concludes, "James counts on our taking toward his main persons attitudes that we cannot take without losing our finer moral sense." Mr. Leavis thus raises fundamental questions. Was James in fact unaware of the evil which appears to be in the basic situation of his characters? If not, how did he propose to relate it to the Utopian fable which Mr. Anderson demonstrates?

With regard to the first question, Mr. Leavis is, I think, mistaken: James knew very well that his tale had sordid aspects. It was his custom to take situations from real life as the starting points for his fictions, and we know that the three late novels employ persons or situations he knew, or had heard about, in this way. The brute facts with which he started often struck him as sordid and meaningless. He explains in the preface to *The Ambassadors,* for instance, that the triteness of Strether's situation, that of the middle-aged provincial who goes to Paris to "see life" for the first time, caused him the greatest difficulty in writing that novel. The difficulty, of course, was to reveal the deeper meaning which he wished to show, in a situation which was literally so hackneyed. The situation in *The Golden Bowl,* the marriage of an American heiress to a titled and philandering European, is equally hackneyed; James could hardly have missed that point. And as Mr. Leavis himself says, James stresses the venality again and again: he never lets us forget the power of Adam Verver's money, behind the majestic social forms, and the sensitive manners, of his characters. James knew what he was doing, in his own terms, at least. Perhaps Mr. Leavis's distaste is due to the fact that James does not admire the "finer moral sense" as he does: if Mr. Anderson is right, Henry junior mistrusted all socially-embodied moral codes just as his father did.

The second question, how James proposes to lead the reader from the unvarnished facts of the story to their deeper meaning—which is nothing less than the saving power of love—has been answered in principle by James himself, in his prefaces, and by his many acute exegetes from Percy Lubbock to R. P. Blackmur. He will, as usual, reveal the hidden motivations of his characters by his dramatic method, which consists in presenting them as directly as possible, in the very act of making their choices, yielding to their temptations, or accepting a deepening vision of their plight and its possibilities. The movement of the novel will consist in the expansion of the central characters' awareness, and what they see— on "the beautiful circuit and subterfuge of their thought and desire"—will gradually lead the reader to see the form and meaning of the whole drama. Thus in *The Golden Bowl* the reader is led, in many repeated but varied figures, from what Fanny Assingham can see, with her myopic worldly shrewdness, to what the Prince sees, with the eye of the natural man, to what Maggie sees as love gradually enlightens her.

The principle of this method, "technique as discovery," as Mr. Mark Schorer calls it, has been known to devotees of James for a long time. But now Mr. Anderson shows us the relation between this fictional technique and the elder James's philosophy. I have called his philosophy a scenario: the myth, or plot, of Western history, and at the same time the plot of the individual's struggle for freedom and enlightenment. The elder

James's philosophy is thus itself dramatic in essence—not so much a static scheme as a counsel of change and movement. For Henry the elder thought that every individual had to experience the main phases of human life in his own way, and as the result of his own unique impulses. Hence his rejection of all rationalized and socially-embodied codes as the ultimate guide to action, and hence his belief in the supreme value of individual freedom and spontaneity. Like his son, he looked to the true artist, and to the woman of good will, as our guides, for he thought that they best preserved candor of perception, truth to feeling, in our world of convention and rationalized forms. Thus if Henry junior were to write a fictional representation of his father's philosophy, at the same time obeying its principles in the poetic act itself, he would create a unique situation, truly individual characters, and, in short, a novel which would stand on its own feet. The philosophy would not be expounded in general terms, or even recognized as somehow "real" apart from the story; it would be (as one might put it) completely absorbed in the concrete instance.

If the relation between the father's philosophy and the son's technique of fiction is as Mr. Anderson describes it, it appears that Henry junior was an even more self-conscious craftsman than we had thought. We must now attribute to him not only the awareness of the scrupulous artist, but some of the awareness of the "thinker" as well.

With this in mind, let us look once more at the novel, this time trying to see the motivation which emerges from a closer acquaintance with the text itself. It has not been sufficiently pointed out that the novel is a struggle for power. The power in question is, literally and in the beginning, that of Adam Verver's vast wealth; and the question is, who shall control it, and to what end? We must think of the Ververs, when we first meet them, as somewhat puzzled to know what to do with their magic millions. They seem to "have everything," and yet, as Maggie says to her father, they are great only if they act on it, not if they don't. Their groping for the proper, the significant, use of vast wealth leads them to their marriages and the struggles that follow. They are the natural prey of Fanny Assingham, who makes her bid for power by arranging the marriages, and then defending them by preserving the forms and appearances which conceal the Prince's affair with Charlotte. The Prince and Charlotte make their claim on power when they reject Fanny's guidance, and attempt to deceive the Ververs by pampering them. Maggie is obliged to grasp power herself when she sees through the deception. To save her husband, she must defeat Charlotte, and that she does in the great scene between the two women at Fawns. She wins the cruel battle in the dark by outdoing Charlotte at her own game of deceit; never letting her know that she knows, and at the same time letting the Prince discover both her knowledge and her forgiveness. Charlotte, helpless and in the dark, has no choice but to obey Adam Verver—and the images of the caged animal and the silken rope, which James uses in this sequence, refer to the power of Adam's money when it is guided by Maggie's vision of love. Thus the reader is led to see the struggle for power in deeper and deeper perspective, and for higher and higher stakes. The power is there, and the evil associated with it: James has not let his own sense of it "slip into abeyance." But he leads the reader to see the power of love at the moment of deepest darkness.

When I paid my quick visit to *The Golden Bowl* twenty years ago I was much struck by the fact that its basic scheme is parallel to that of French neoclassic tragedy, Racine's for example. James does not, like his contemporary British novelists, portray Edwardian society for its own sake; he uses its forms and appearances as a means of revealing the perilous life of the spirit in the severe light of the moral intellect; and in that he is more French than English. The substance of *The Golden Bowl*, like that of neoclassic tragedy, is a debate on moral issues, and the cast of characters is arranged in such a way as to develop the debate on several levels. Thus Fanny Assingham serves, like a Racinian *confidante*, to point out, with shrewdness and logic, all the considerations of worldly prudence. Maggie corresponds to a Phèdre or Bérénice: in the end she rejects Fanny's wisdom because she has learned to act on wider premises, just as Racine's heroines leave their sharp-witted advisers behind when they are ready for the gloomy heroism of their deepest insights.

I still believe that this view of *The Golden Bowl* will take us a certain distance toward understanding it. James's famous scruples are akin to the cruel clarity of French moralists, and his dramaturgy owes a great deal to his lifelong cult of the Comédie Française. But in the light of Mr. Anderson's allegorical scheme, this comparison may be corrected and made more precise. In *The Golden Bowl* James was not presenting a purely rational ethic like that of the age of Racine and Descartes; that is what he was doing in *The Ambassadors*, wherein poor Strether is caught in the very Racinian contradiction between the glamour of worldly passion and his reasoned duty. Perhaps that is why the novel is laid in Paris, the city of refined passion and rational light. The ambience of *The Golden Bowl* is wider and softer, its setting is London, dim seat of empire, and Fawns, the mild-majestic country house. And as we now see, the action moves from reason and the moral will to a kind of religious humanism in which love is supposed to transcend the paradoxes of rationality. Moreover, *The Golden Bowl* has a historic dimension which neoclassic tragedy lacks. The ethical world of Racine is timeless, above history; it makes very little difference to his action whether Bérénice inhabits ancient Rome or seventeenth-century France. But in *The Golden Bowl* the differences between the Prince's Rome, modern London, and America, now and in promise, constitute a crucial aspect of the theme.

The historic dimension of the novel may be described as the theme of empire, or rule, with its connotations of worry and glory. I have said that the drama is a struggle for power within one family; but through the London setting, the Ververs' vast power of wealth, and the Prince's Roman tradition, James makes this private struggle suggest the westward course of Empire, toward the New Jerusalem which America should ideally mean. In the first sentence of the book, when we are introduced to the Prince as he takes his walk through London on the eve of his marriage to Maggie, we read, "The Prince was one of the modern Romans who find by the Thames a more convincing image of the truth of the ancient state than any they have left by the Tiber. . . . If it was a question of an Imperium, he said to himself, and if one wished, as a Roman, to recover a little the sense of that, the place to do so was on London Bridge." Empire has taken its course, long since, from Rome to London, and now in London it is the American rich whom the Prince finds assuming the imperium in their turn. And he will find, as he is slowly trained for the job of Prince-consort, that the American imperium, based on the power of money, is more terrifying and more loving than he had thought.

It is the historical dimension of *The Golden Bowl*, derived in part from the elder James, but originally realized in the novel, which led me to say that the work recalls Vergil, Dante, the late Shakespeare, in their idealized interpretations of history. Is not James, in this novel, trying to imagine a historic mission for the "innocent" American spirit, as Vergil did for the Roman genius in the *Aeneid?* The relationships James presents between the moral will and the power to love suggest certain elements in the middle and end of the *Purgatorio*, where Dante treats rational morality and Christian love in the context of a Christian philosophy of history. And the suggested course of empire from Rome to Britain reminds me of *Cymbeline,* especially the natural-humane-religious reconciliations with which it ends. Of course these comparisons must be taken lightly. James is not one of the greatest. But I think he inherited a belated echo of their themes.

I must add that the picture of America which the novel gives is not only the New Jerusalem, the Swedenborgian Golden Age. We also see it as "the great alkali desert of cheap divorce," and as spiritually starved by its debauch of heartless Titanism. Maggie's innocent love, like Milly Theale's, is a providential compensation for American materialism, as Mr. Anderson points out. James certainly wants to give an ideal interpretation of America, yet at the same time he was struggling realistically with actual problems of culture and politics. Some of these have made the headlines since World War II: since this country, with its vast power of money, has been trying to assume imperial responsibilities in Europe without losing faith in its own innocent good will. James wrote *The Golden Bowl* more than fifty years ago, but in that half century it has come to seem, more and more, a parable for our times. How wrong Mr. Leavis was when he wrote of James, "His genius . . . was not the explorer's or the pioneer's, and it had nothing prophetic about it."

Such are some of the things I seem to make out on a second visit to *The Golden Bowl,* with the aid of Mr. Anderson's study. We can see, I think, more than before, the relation between James the artist and James the prophetic thinker. But after all our analysis the final question of the success of the novel as a work of art remains, to be answered by each reader according to his own taste. Is it a poetic masterpiece, as Mr. Blackmur believes, or is Mr. Leavis right after all, that it marks a queer degeneration in James, a loss of grip on language and reality? This brings me once more to the nature of

James's allegory, for in that, I think, lies the peculiar flavor of the late works.

I can sympathize to some degree with those who do not like the late manner. It is a little ghostly, a voice which pleads too much, too elaborately, perhaps in vain. We think of James's lifelong isolation, his celibacy, his position between America and Europe, where he saw what no audience could quite see. He did not earn the detachment of age, like Dante or Shakespeare, by working through human love and a human community, but found himself in it too soon; and so, we may guess, he forfeited the immediate authority, the concrete weight, of the ultimate masters. But *The Ambassadors, The Wings of the Dove* and *The Golden Bowl* do correspond to the late works of the masters. Mr. Anderson rightly calls this trilogy "the divine novel," implying an analogy to the *Divine Comedy*. It is, for James, what *The Tempest* was for Shakespeare, a work in which he was no longer groping, but presenting the quintessence of his view of human life. Late works of this kind seem to be naturally allegorical. The double-take of allegory, the vision seen for a second time and against a meaning which somehow transcends it, seems to come with age, when the spirit, freed from its own private obsessions, still lives and sees. *The Golden Bowl,* whether one likes it or not, must be judged as a late work of this kind.

Mr. Anderson, coming to the end of his superb study, offers his view of the final value of James's art: "There are no problems in James's universe," he writes. "In the end James is not a tragic poet but the poet of his father's theodicy." It is here that I cannot quite follow Mr. Anderson. He himself has given us the clue to a better understanding of the relation between the theodicy and the art. And, in general, he implies too sharp a contradiction between an ordered philosophic view and a tragic sense of human life. *The Divine Comedy* ends in "that heaven which most receives God's light," but do we feel therefore that a tragic sense of human destiny is lacking in the poem? Aeschylus's trilogy on the House of Atreus ends with the affirmation of an ideal order, but we cannot for that reason deny it the name of tragedy. *The Golden Bowl* in the actual reading feels tragic to me throughout. There is tragedy in the Prince's and Charlotte's destined passion; in Maggie's solitary vision of evil; in her cruel struggle with Charlotte. The underlying movement of the novel is problematic, dark and frightened, for all the urbanity of its surfaces. And in the moments when the ideal order of love is briefly glimpsed I do not find that James suggests that the tragic quality of life has hereby been made unreal.

Consider the very end of the novel, in which the allegorical scheme is completed. Mr. Verver and Charlotte briefly visit Maggie and the Prince on their way through London to America. The Principino makes his appearance, and is removed by his nurse. The Ververs depart, and Maggie and the Prince are left alone. The allegorical meaning of this episode is that divine wisdom (Mr. Verver) has taken the evil-idolized human self (Charlotte) into captivity, thus freeing divine love (Maggie) to consummate marriage with natural man (the Prince). The baby Principino represents the humanity to come, divine-natural man. But how does this episode feel in the actual reading? It feels very much as a moment of crisis in any marriage—a crisis just successfully passed— might feel. In any marriage which lasts a while there may be moments when an ideal love is briefly glimpsed, and of course the sharper such fleeting intuitions of felicity are, all defenseless in the midst of family life, the more terror they bring with them. So it proves for the Prince and Maggie. At the very end the Prince, holding Maggie in his arms, at a loss for words, echoes their fragmentary conversation as follows: "'See? I see nothing but you.' And the truth of it had, with this force, after a moment, so strangely lighted his eyes, that, as for pity and dread of them, she buried her own in his breast."

It seems to me that the authentic tragic emotion (pity and dread, as James puts it) is here, in the instant of vision and fulfillment itself. The allegorical meaning may be found there also, once Mr. Anderson has given us the clue, for it has been built into the whole course of the narrative, its symbols and relationships, its characters, even their names. But James does not violate the immediate effect of his poem or fiction by the allegory. The characters are imagined as in the midst of life, with its familiar darkness and peril, its transience and mortality. Maggie may represent the Eden to come at that moment, but only as a real person might briefly and mysteriously feel it. Thus one may read the novel as a criticism of the philosophy it so strangely embodies—a comment upon the metaphysical status of any ideal scheme.

We must conclude that James's allegorical method in *The Golden Bowl* is unique. It is not what Dante calls the "allegory of poets," in which the concepts of moral philosophy are personified—the type of allegory we associate with *Pilgrim's Progress*. Nor is it Dante's "allegory of theologians," for that is based upon analogies between men and their history and their world on one side, and God, the transcendent object of faith, on the other. The thought behind *The Golden Bowl*, as we now see, is the elder James's antiphilosophic philosophy, which is also a religion without God in the classic Christian sense; "God," in that scheme, exists only within man. No wonder James devoted such passionate intensity to imagining his people in life, actual human life, for the only reality and divinity he recognized was there. They remain, nevertheless, a bit ghostly—"poetic," as Mr. Blackmur puts it—like Dante's Vergil and Statius on the third day of the purgatorial climb, the realm of high humanism. But James's people, creations of the moral imagination as they are, must carry a weight of hope and faith traditionally reserved for God. No wonder Maggie is filled with dread when the Prince, in the passage I quoted, turns to her for all his light and love. She cannot tell him to refrain, as Dante's Vergil does when Statius mistakes him for the goal of human life:

> Frate,
> non far, chè tu se'ombra, ed ombra vedi.

Maggie does not have a God to refer the Prince to, any more than James did. James was attempting the imaginative feat of suggesting a meaning in Western history and in human life without benefit of an objectified system of philosophy or religion. The mere attempt, however we may judge its success, throws light on our contemporary problems of art, and upon the relation between our pragmatic American tradition and the main line of European culture. It is the great value of Mr. Anderson's work that it leads us to consider James in this way—a new theme for devotees of the master to explore and to discuss.

Kenneth Burke's *Grammar of Motives**

THE *Grammar of Motives* is the first part of Mr. Burke's work on the arts of language, to be followed by a *Symbolic* and a *Rhetoric*. Mr. Burke demands, as he tells us, "a fully worked-out version of the ways of *homo dialecticus*," and what he demands he here provides. The peculiar property of the Grammar is that it illuminates many kinds of attempts (sociological, philosophic, psychological) to talk about human motives: it operates Socratically to assist many half-formed theories to become self-conscious and articulate. It continually anticipates what the reader feels he was about to say to himself; or, as Mr. Mark Van Doren puts it, "I have thought much about this, but seldom with the benefit of his sharpness." The reader finds it difficult at last to tell just where his thought begins and Mr. Burke's ends. The present review is written from a point of view which Mr. Burke would probably not recognize as "grammatical" at all; yet the Grammar has done much to clarify it.

Mr. Burke sets forth his general subject and method as follows: "The book is concerned with the forms of thought which, in accordance with the nature of the world as all men necessarily experience it, are exemplified in the attributing of motives. . . . [These forms of

---

* *A Grammar of Motives*, by Kenneth Burke, Prentice-Hall, Inc., 1945.

thought] are equally present in systematically elaborated metaphysical structures, in legal judgments, in poetry and fiction, in political and scientific works, in news and in bits of gossip offered at random. We shall use five terms as generating principles of our investigation. They are Act, Scene, Agent, Agency and Purpose. . . . Any complete statement about motives will offer *some kind* of answer to these five questions."

This quotation shows how similar Mr. Burke's point of view is to that of Kant in *The Critique of Pure Reason.* His method is somewhat more empirical: he offers dialectical analyses of various writings which "attribute motives"; but he shows thereby the ineluctable claims of his basic forms of thought or "five terms," as well as the failure of the reason ever to reach finality or completeness in its account of motives.

The *Grammar* may also be compared with a more recent and much-neglected work: Professor Scott Buchanan's *Poetry and Mathematics.* This is a study (suggestive rather than complete) of analogies between the abstract forms of poetry and the abstract forms of mathematics: of the ultimate forms of thought which govern our particular enquiries and our building of metaphysical, scientific and poetic structures.

Both Mr. Burke and Professor Buchanan see the efforts of reason as perpetually doomed to partial failure, and the life of the mind as a never-completed process or succession of acts. It is thus tragic, or comic, and the form of drama is in a sense regarded by both as the most fundamental form of all. Mr. Burke's five terms are, as he says, "dramatistic," and he would probably agree with Professor Buchanan that "drama, at its best, undercuts the scientific and religious habit of mind," and "consequently the best metaphysical criticism of mathematics and poetry is to be found in the drama and the novel." But these authors are both concerned with terms, concepts, forms of *thought;* and (perhaps because of this focus of interest) they tend to *identify* drama and dialectic. One of the questions I wish to raise about the *Grammar* is the relations between Mr. Burke's dialectical method and the more direct imitation of motivated humans which is "drama at its best."

The other question I wish to raise is closely related to the question of drama versus dramatism. Mr. Burke points out that the project of a *grammar* of motives, the analysis of *terms*, is essentially rationalistic. Yet the key term in his analysis is Act, or Action, or, as he sometimes calls it, Act-Substance; and this term is derived from the Realist philosophies of Aristotle and Aquinas. The attempt to submit it to the authority of the Reason as rationalistically conceived seems to me at best too limiting, at worst very confusing. In what sense, or to what extent, can there be a *grammar* of actions?

"Act-Substance" and Grammar

The first part of the book is called "Ways of Placement," and it is divided into three sections, Container and Thing Contained, Antinomies of Definition, and Scope and Reduction. In Container and Thing Contained Mr. Burke explains and illustrates from several plays his five terms, especially Act and Scene. He shows how, in the attempt to formulate motives, one is led dialectically from Act to Scene to Agent—how any of the five terms may be "reduced" to one or more of the others. Behaviorism for instance reduces Act to Scene: that is, it interprets human motivation as mechanical response to the physical environment, thereby neglecting essential and inescapable perspectives. "Insofar as men cannot themselves create the universe," Mr. Burke explains, "there must remain something essentially enigmatic about the problem of motives," and "this underlying enigma will manifest itself in inevitable ambiguities and inconsistencies among the terms for motives. Accordingly, what we want is *not terms that avoid ambiguity,* but *terms that clearly reveal the strategic spots at which ambiguities necessarily arise."*

The five terms define the rules or conditions of the reason's attempt to define Act-Substance, which, as I remarked, is the key term for motives. In Antinomies of Definition Mr. Burke runs over the characteristic moves which the reason makes in its efforts to fix its slippery antagonist, trying "contextual definition" and "familial definition" and tangling with the paradoxes of the intrinsic and the extrinsic. From this encounter Act-Substance emerges victorious: undefined but indispensable. Mr. Burke has affirmed its centrality, and our need for it, in any attempt to define motives. He has defended it against several of its most trenchant critics, from Locke to Bertrand Russell. He has had many illuminating things to say about act as this concept figures in Aristotle and Aquinas, pointing out its integral connections with Potency, Form, Matter and Substance. But this is a crucial point in the development of the *Grammar.* "Grammar" must be philosophically neutral, without ontological commitments: it must remain at a level of abstraction higher than that of metaphysics. Act-Substance must be considered as a form of thought or limiting concept only, in complete abstraction from particular Act-Substances, or beings. "One might hypothetically grant that the treatment of motives in terms of 'action' and 'substance' is wholly fallacious," Mr. Burke writes; "yet defend it as central to the placement of *statements* about motives." In short, Mr. Burke requires this concept, yet cannot proceed from it to any of the *things* it signifies, lest he move from thought to experience and the dialectical process come to a pause.

In Scope and Reduction Mr. Burke treats Act-Substance conceptually, showing how the concept *in abstracto* is ultimately inconceivable. He starts, as it would appear, Realistically, with a "Representative Anecdote" which is itself not conceptual or "logical" at all —God's Act of Creation. "We are saying that to study the nature of the term, Act, one must select a prototype or paradigm of action. This prototype we find in the conception of a perfect or total act, such as the 'Act of Creation.'" But we soon see that this "act" is convenient for Mr. Burke's purposes not only because we cannot conceive it, but also because we cannot possibly have any direct experience of it. It is the *term* we are investigating, and in this case terms are all we have. We are, from the first, in the realm of the conceptual only. To call the Creation an *anecdote* ("a narrative, usually brief, of . . . an event of curious interest, told without malice and usually with intent to amuse or please") has also the rhetorical effect of reducing medieval theology to the logically absurd, and delightful, world of Molièreesque comedy. By these strategies "grammar" is saved; but what has become of the notion of Action? Dialectically assaulted, so to speak, at the ultimate level of abstraction, it has completely disappeared.

The theologians of the Middle Ages were careful to point out that we never could conceive the Act of Creation. Such remote understanding of it as they tried to reach was by analogy only. The theological question is perhaps unimportant in this context, but it seems to me that the nature of the concept of Action is a fundamental puzzle in Mr. Burke's scheme. Action is an analogical concept, and in Scope and Reduction Mr. Burke treats it as though it were univocal. In general, he does not use the notion of analogy in this book, for analogy assumes some direct perception of real things and their relationships, while the *Grammar* is strictly confined to the definition and transformation of our *concepts*.

The Thomistic doctrine of analogy (according to Penido and Maritain) distinguishes it both from univocity and from equivocation. Father Penido explains, in his *De L'Analogie*:

D'une manière très générale, toute analogie suppose deux conditions ontologiques: 1° une pluralité réelle

d'êtres, et donc entre ces êtres une diversité essentielle—
le Monisme est l'ennemi-né de l'Analogie; 2° au sein de
cette multiplicité, de cette inégalité, une certaine unité.

The analogical concept (unlike the univocal concepts
of rationalism, which are clear and distinct in themselves) is not completely abstracted, and hence cannot
be understood unless the eye of the mind is kept, so to
speak, upon the beings to which the concept refers.
"Action" cannot be understood or properly handled ab-
stractly. We can develop our knowledge of it, accumu-
late a lore, through the study of particular actions. Yet
in spite of its dangers and difficulties, the notion of
analogy seems to me indispensable for the understanding
of human motivation in the widest sense. The *Divine
Comedy,* for example, represents poetically and dramatically many acts which are analogous. The *Grammar*
would not provide the clue to Dante's composition; and
rational or grammatical motivation is a moment only in
the hierarchy of human acts which Dante the pilgrim
traverses. This moment recurs "by analogy" at many
levels of the ascent, and is most completely developed
in the central cantos of the *Purgatorio,* when the pilgrim encounters the antinomies of definition which interest Mr. Burke: Action-Passion, Freedom-Determinism,
Knowledge-Will, and the like. It is transcended when
the soul accepts the limitations of reason, and gets a
sense of the analogies between its life and the lives of
other creatures:

Every substantial form, which is distinct from matter
and is in union with it, has a specific virtue contained
within itself
Which is not perceived save in operation, nor is manifested except by its effects, just as life in a plant by the
green leaves.

I do not wish to imply that Mr. Burke deifies reason.
On the contrary, his dialectic is a continual demonstra-

tion of the limitations as well as the resources of reason. Moreover, he often explains very clearly the inherent limitations of a grammar of motives, as for instance when he says that his study of action is limited to action as rational, i.e., to conceptual thought. The second part of his book is called "The Philosophical Schools," and here his method is completely adequate to the vast material.

Our problem in this section is to consider seven primary philosophic languages in terms of the pentad. . . . In treating the various schools as languages, we may define their substantial relationship to one another by deriving them from a common terminological ancestor. . . . Any of the terms may be seen in terms of the others. . . . Dramatistically, the different schools are to be distinguished by the fact that each school features a different one of the five terms.

On this basis they are classified as follows:

For the featuring of scene, the corresponding terminology is materialism.

For the featuring of agent, the corresponding terminology is idealism.

For the featuring of agency, the corresponding terminology is pragmatism.

For the featuring of purpose, the corresponding terminology is mysticism.

For the featuring of act, the corresponding terminology is realism.

It is clear from this scheme that the adherents of each school will object: I have already indicated my reservations about Mr. Burke's treatment of the realistic concept of "act." But there is nothing to prevent one's enjoying Mr. Burke's treatment of other schools; and what he does with materialism, pragmatism, and idealism seems to me superb. These schools still dominate our intellectual life, not only overt philosophizing, but thinking of all kinds. Mr. Burke's dialectical analysis of their terminologies or basic forms of thought is Aristotelian in spirit. His five terms operate rather like Aristotle's four causes, which enable him to account for the analogous schools of his time without completely dismissing any of them. Mr. Burke enables one to read the modern schools at once sympathetically and critically, and to see them in relation to each other.

The key to his success is in his use of Action. This notion, now limited to the action of the soul as rational, returns to dominate the scene. He is enabled to see the various schools in a wider context than any of them recognizes, by considering "the different kinds of *assertion* which the different schools would exemplify in a hypothetical state of purity." It is the assertion, or action, which his dialectical analysis of their languages reveals. "We believe that an explicit approach to language as a dialectical structure admonishes us both what to look for and what to look out for, as regards the ways of symbolic action (and no statement about motives can be anything other than symbolic action)." Mr. Burke does indeed work dialectically, forewarning us and forearming us against this dangerous art; but so effectively that the substantial world behind it is always clearly implied. He masters dialectic so completely that he points beyond it, to the unwritten drama or comedy of contemporary life.

Dialectic and Drama

The last part of the *Grammar* is entitled "On Dialectic." Mr. Burke studies this art first, as in his custom, by means of a Representative Anecdote, "The Dialectic of Constitutions." After an interesting explanation of his choice of this "anecdote," he offers luminous analyses of the languages of constitution-makers, jurists who interpret constitutions, and social theorists who write about them in their historic contexts. His eye is on the efforts of "homo dialecticus," but as usual he sees him so clearly that the reader divines that animal as political also, raising the shaky mental artifact of the Res Publica upon the anomalous "ground" of the diverse and changing ways of life of modern populations. Behind the abstract devising of the American Constitution in the age of the Enlightenment are the older, half-unavowed religious and moral traditions; behind subsequent efforts to interpret it rationally is the environment which science so rapidly transforms. Mr. Burke's remarkable accomplishment is to throw light upon the real scene and the real protagonists, while austerely limiting himself to his dialectical art, the analysis of rationalizing.

But what exactly is the "stance" which he takes up in order to gain these insights and these perspectives? He is a dialectician who cleans up after himself so well, as he goes along, that both dialectic and dialectician have disappeared when all is over. The only thing which I find disquieting about this magic is that drama disappears too—as though the substantial development of Tragedy, or of Dante's *via purgativa,* were only another instance of the dialectical transformation of *terms.* It is in the last section of the book, "On Dialectic in General," that Mr. Burke comes close to dealing directly with such questions as I am endeavoring to raise. And here he seems to be saying definitely that drama is only a form of dialectic, dramatic development essentially terminological. He illustrates this view, first, by a long and very illuminating analysis of the *Phaedrus,* with special reference to the transformations of the term Love. He then considers more briefly several works of fiction and drama, including *Death in Venice, Remembrance of Things Past,* and *Peer Gynt.* All these works are quests for a way of life, and hence exhibit transformations; but it is my thesis that neither their content nor their principles of composition can be understood purely dialectically. Behind Mr. Burke's view of the dialectic process there lurks ritual drama, much as medieval or Aristotelian Realism is lurking behind his account of the action of the rational soul.

The Platonic dialogues are certainly the *locus classicus* for the study of the relation between drama and dialectic. The direct, histrionic sense which we gain of Socrates and Phaedrus themselves, prior to our aquaintance with their thinking, would seem to be dramatic rather than dialectical. But we see them at a particular moment only in the rhythm of human development: they are caught in the act of thinking. Apart from their mild flirtation, their actions are rational only; and though their ideas change, they do not. Socrates is at his spiritual summit when the dialogue opens, and as for Phaedrus, is he not like those contemporary sad young men who "understand" Bach and Plato to no avail? Contrast this with the transformation represented in *Oedipus Rex*. Oedipus's ideas are certainly different at the end of the play from what they were at the beginning, but the change in his ideas appears to result, not from thinking, but from suffering and direct experience—a development of the man himself. This transformation is shown in the whole tragic rhythm of "Purpose to Passion to Perception," or, as Mr. Burke calls it in this book, Poiema-Pathema-Mathema. Plato's drama of thought may have an abstract shape like that of tragedy, but he envisages a different Act-Substance or actualization: the soul as conceptualizing and verbalizing, instead of the creature responding as a whole to a "total situation." In short, if the *Phaedrus* is a drama, it is, as such, a more limited genre than tragedy proper, and the reduction of its transformations to the transformation of terms, whether proper or not, misses the essential property of ritual tragedy. Mr. Burke himself, in his *Philosophy of Literary Form,* proposed to take "ritual drama as the hub," or as he would now put it the Representative Anecdote. It is significant that for the purposes of his *Grammar* he should substitute the Enlightened anecdote of the modern Constitution, for the Realist anecdote of Greek tragedy.

In the analyses of Proust, Mann and Ibsen, Mr. Burke "substitutes" works of art whose content and principles of composition may be called (with qualifications) subjective-idealist. Aschenbach finds in his dream of Venice (a "circle closed on the outside"), at the end of his quest and its transformations, a narcissistic-homosexual *Liebestod* which is Wagnerian rather than Platonic or Tragic. Proust finds the pseudo-beatitude of remembered feeling. As for Peer, who is more objectively *represented* than the others, he ends, with a sigh of relief, in the near-nonentity of childhood in Solveig's maternal lap. To say, as Mr. Burke does, that at this moment Peer is "translated to the role of the Christ-child, whose conception was an Annunciation," seems to me grotesque. The analogy is much closer to "the role" of Mrs. Solness's "nine lovely dolls": the fetish of a woman's thwarted and in-turned love. It is in his account of these works that Mr. Burke's method and attitude produces its least satisfactory results. He is looking at the over-all shape and at the purely abstract formal relations within the work; and from this point of view there are similarities between the Tragic Rhythm, the *via purgativa,* and any process of change whatever. But the crucial questions about works of fiction and drama, which are composed of concrete elements, are missed entirely at this level of abstraction. The crucial questions have to do with the *being* which the artist envisages, and the histrionic, rather than rational, action whereby he imitates or represents it.

Mr. Burke explains that the proper material for revealing the *Grammar* of motives is metaphysics, jurisprudence, and, in general, essentially rational or conceptual arts. In the *Symbolic* and *Rhetoric* which are to follow he will consider primarily poetry, fiction and drama. I hope that in those works he will return to what he has called "Poetic Realism"—a way of the mind's life which is not reducible either to dialectic or to the subjective symbolism and "qualitative progressions" of the idealist tradition.

Meanwhile the *Grammar* is our indispensable guide to the ubiquitous operations of "homo dialecticus" in the actual world of applied science, bureaucracy, money, and abstract principles. It is the sign of Mr. Burke's extraordinary vitality that he is always victoriously engaging the public languages of our time; of his artistic integrity that he does so by the strict practice of dialectic. There are many who share his point of view, but few if any who have worked out such a discipline to effectuate it. And, while confining himself to dialectic, he curiously transcends it. He says in his introduction that he was led to write the *Grammar* through work on a theory of comedy. The comic inspiration is never lost. He shows us the rational mind hopelessly but eternally committed to the definition of human motives, much as Molière shows us Arnolphe, in *The School for Wives,* frantically seeking the logical control of Love. The plight of these heroes is rendered laughable to their audiences, not through tragic or purgatorial transcendence—not because we are invited to occupy a substantially different stance—but through "comic transcendence," through the delightful clarity with which the perpetual-motion machine of their intrigues is presented.

Two Perspectives on European Literature

THESE two books,* now available in Mr. Willard R. Trask's excellent translations, have both already had distinguished careers in their original German. Auerbach's *Mimesis* was published in 1946, Curtius's *Latin Middle Ages* in 1948. Both emerge from what the Germans call *Philologie*—the study of language so defined as to include not only the chief tongues of our tradition at least, but also all the arts of letters, philosophy, history, anthropology, and "culture." A philologist in this sense must have learned Greek, Latin, and the modern languages of Europe at an early age; he must have labored for many years thereafter at his researches and general reading; and he must be blessed with the stamina to survive the attacks of his equally learned colleagues, who also lay claim to all the available knowledge. We do not have anything quite like this tradition in our country; students of literature over here are usually obliged to improvise their learning as they go along, on the basis of poor early education. Even our most

* *European Literature and the Latin Middle Ages*, by Ernst Robert Curtius, Bollingen Series XXXVI, Pantheon, 1953. *Mimesis, the Representation of Reality in Western Literature*, by Erich Auerbach, Princeton University Press, 1953.

intransigent "scholars"—those who pretend with the straightest faces to scientific rigor and exhaustiveness— are timid and relaxed in comparison with a fully-developed *Philolog* of the good period, the period which ended with Hitler.

But both of these books are more than science and specialized learning. They are motivated, in their very different ways, by an interest in the art of literature. For that reason they have much to say to anyone seriously interested in that art: one may think of them as climbing, bloody but still breathing, from the arena of *Wissenschaft,* to address a more general audience. That is why there may be some point in my attempting to review them. The record of the professional battles which these books have survived is in learned journals all over the Western world; now, I hope, they will be read (as I read them) in the spirit of the enquiring amateur.

The first thing to say about them is that they are entirely different from each other, in the materials they investigate, their methods and purposes, and in the taste and philosophy of their authors.

I

Professor Curtius was known until Hitler as the great German critic of modern French literature, and also as one of the first and most important contributors to Eliot's *Criterion.* Both a connoisseur and a practitioner of the arts of letters, he has translated Eliot, Gide, Valéry and Jorge Guillén, among others. He is one of those who stood for European literature in the exciting and tragic period between the wars, the period to which we owe so much: a time when the Goethean notion of Europe as a concert was briefly revived. Nazism and the approach of World War II put an end to that period, and to Professor Curtius's immediate concern with contemporary literature. As early as 1932, in his anti-Nazi book *Deutscher Geist in Gefahr,* he "pleaded," as he tells us in the foreword to the English edition of *The Latin Middle Ages,* "for a new Humanism, which should integrate the Middle Ages from Augustine to Dante." He continues, describing the *raison d'être* of his book:

When the German catastrophe came, I decided to serve the idea of a medievalistic Humanism by studying the Latin literature of the Middle Ages. These studies occupied me for fifteen years. The result is the present book . . . not the product of purely scholarly interests, it grew out of a concern for the preservation of Western culture. It seeks to serve an understanding of the Western cultural tradition in so far as it is manifested in literature. It attempts to illuminate the unity of that tradition in space and time by the application of new methods. In the intellectual chaos of the present it has become necessary, and happily not impossible, to demonstrate that unity. But the demonstration can only be made from a universal standpoint. Such a standpoint is afforded by Latinity. Latin was the language of the educated during the thirteen centuries which lie between Vergil and Dante.

To this explanation one should add a remark from a lecture of Curtius's, *The Medieval Bases of Western Thought,* also reprinted in the English edition: "The lesson of the Middle Ages is reverent reception and faithful transmission of a precious deposit. This is also the lesson which we may draw from Dante."

These explanations show how the reader should approach the six hundred closely printed pages of the vast work; without them he might easily be lost. Professor Curtius studies the Middle Ages as the period when European literature was, in fact, one; and also for the clues they may offer us for the reception and transmission of the literary heritage. He focuses upon literature in the strictest sense—not philosophy, or religion, or theology, but the arts of language approximately as the ancient rhetoricians understood them. Professor Curtius is thus still concerned with European as distinguished from national or period literature, just as he was as a critic of modern French; but now he seeks the root, and he proposes to develop methods of investigation and analysis more like those of the medieval Latinists than like those of the modern critic. The plan is both imaginative and austere—an *askesis* which Curtius undergoes, and then prescribes for modern letters in general.

We have had in recent years in this country a revival of interest in traditional rhetoric. A book like Sister Miriam Joseph's study of Shakespeare's arts of language comes to mind—or, from quite a different point of view, Mr. Kenneth Burke's fertile efforts to rethink some of the concepts of ancient rhetoric for modern use. Professor Curtius's study is related to both of these works, but different in its basic intention from either. Sister Miriam Joseph is concerned only with Shakespeare's use of the traditional arts of language, while Curtius, not primarily concerned with any particular author, seeks to illuminate the lore itself, when it was the common property of educated Europe. He does not, like Mr. Burke, apply his finding to modern works, but suggests in principle and in a few examples how the vernacular literatures did in fact grow out of the common Latin root.

Moreover, Professor Curtius regards literature in his strict sense as a more fundamental and indestructible bearer of the whole cultural tradition than philosophy or religion. This view of literature is cognate with his Humanism, which leaves room for both Cicero and Goethe: literature forms men's minds, and by its means the basis of civilized life is transmitted from one generation to the next. He thinks of Homer as the beginning, and Goethe as the last worthy representative, of Western culture as a unity. For that reason his study of medieval Latinity includes not only conceptions of form and mechanics from ancient rhetoric, but also recurrent topics and metaphors; governing concepts like the Goddess Natura, the Ideal Landscape, the Muses, all of which define the common *content* of literature. He gives accounts of the evolution of the notion of a classic, the formation of canons, attitudes to Heroes and Rulers, Education, the Book as Symbol, which throw light on the role of literature in the economy of medieval culture as a whole. In three theoretical chapters, on Poetry and Rhetoric, Poetry and Philosophy, and Poetry and Theology respectively, he clarifies his conception of the fundamental role of literature: it is not that he would disregard the issues of philosophy or the problem of belief, but rather that he thinks literature treats them more adequately, and especially more permanently, than the disciplines which aim to erect conceptual systems. In this belief in literature as the central embodiment of the common culture Professor Curtius reaffirms the Humanism which inspired him and many others between the wars—the period of the Weimar Republic, the Entretiens de Pontigny, and the *Criterion*.

Most of the book is devoted to Medieval Latin Literature; not to the analysis of poems, narratives, or plays, but rather to its theoretical basis and common content, as I indicated above. But Professor Curtius always has the vernacular literatures up to the eighteenth century in mind, and from time to time he refers to them, giving brief examples of their growth out of the Latin root. After the main argument, there are twenty-five Excursuses on various topics which enrich the general picture; and there one finds three short essays on Spanish literature, including "Calderón's Theory of Art and the *Artes Liberales*." In these essays he makes it very clear how he conceives the relation between modern European literature and Latinity.

Dante is of course the author who best exemplifies the medieval heritage, the process whereby it was acquired, and its transmission to the vernacular literatures. Professor Curtius mentions Dante in the first chapter, and seems to have him in mind throughout; but he has comparatively little to say about him directly, especially when one reflects how much there would be to say about him. What he does say about Dante is pretty closely confined to Dante's Latinity, in accord with the theme of the book as a whole. He demonstrates that the *Divine Comedy* would not have been possible without that culture. He shows, for example, that the basic scheme of alternating pagan and Christian *exempla* in the *Purgatorio,* though completely digested and re-formed by Dante for his own purposes, was one of the common resources which he inherited. He shows that Dante's Letter to Can Grande, that crucial and (until recently) neglected work in which Dante explains his own methods and principles of composition, can only be understood in the light of the Latinity of the time. He shows that Dante's conception of poetry, especially in his claim of cognitive value for it, was quite unlike that of Aquinas: he sees Dante as poet in contradistinction to the philosopher or theologian. In these respects Dante embodies a tradition older than the Scholasticism of his time, and lasting beyond it. Thus Dante is the prime instance of literature undercutting, as it were, any and all abstract systems. In all of this there is light on Dante —one indispensable perspective, at least, upon that great figure.

Yet the question remains, about Dante and I suppose about medieval Latinity in general, how adequate the cult of Humane Letters is for complete understanding. Professor Curtius of course knows and says that Dante and his period were Christian, but he does not investigate the formative effects of Christian doctrine and belief upon men's minds and arts. We know that Dante's conception of poetry, though not Scholastic, was Christian, and that many of his techniques and formal principles were derived from Scripture and the Hebraic-Christian lore of its interpretation: he tells us so himself, in the same Letter to Can Grande in which he lists the *modi* derived from Latinity. Specialists in various fields —notably Arabic culture—have objected to some aspects of the book on the ground that *their* perspective on the period was left out: the kind of scholarly problems inevitable in a work of this vast scope. Behind it all lurk the insoluble puzzles of history: what does it take to revive Humane Letters? Is a love and understanding of Humane Letters themselves enough, or would it require a faith beyond them to make them sprout once more, like the withered tree in Dante's Paradiso Terrestre, which puts forth spring foliage when Christ's ear touches it? To answer the fundamental questions raised by this book would require vast erudition, plus a prophetic insight which would be even harder to come by.

Lentement les temps se divident: our children's children may see what the fate of Humane Letters is to be. Meanwhile we have in *European Literature and the Latin Middle Ages* a vast store of significant learning, and many new and important insights into the Humane literary heritage and its precarious transmission.

II

Professor Auerbach, now at Yale, has been in this country since the end of the war, and some of his work has been published in *The Hudson Review* and other literary magazines, and in learned journals here. He has published an important work on Dante in German, *Dante als Dichter der Irdischen Welt*, many articles on Romance languages and literatures, and *Figura*, a study of the development of Dante's allegory. *Mimesis*, written in Istanbul during the war, is his most extensive work, and the best one in which to study his original and illuminating methods of literary analysis.

Professor Auerbach studies the representation of reality in twenty chapters, each based on one or more short passages from works of literature, beginning with the *Odyssey* and ending with *To the Lighthouse*. On the way he considers Petronius, two late Latin narratives, three medieval texts, the Farinata-Cavalcante episode from the *Inferno,* bits of Rabelais, Shakespeare and Cervantes; samples of French neoclassic literature, and of Stendhal, Balzac, Flaubert, the Goncourts, and Zola. This slight indication of the contents of the book will show how vast its scope is, and how impossible it would be, even for one with the requisite erudition, to estimate its success in detail. Professor Auerbach's methods make things easy for the reader who lacks much knowledge of Latin style in the Dark Ages, for example: each passage analyzed is short, and the elucidations are very effective. Every chapter is good reading, both because of the light shed on the particular text, and because of the fascination of Professor Auerbach's methods, ostensibly philological *explication de texte,* actually the analysis, in the small example, of the author's basic attitudes to "reality," and of his strategies for representing it. But I will not attempt to discuss it in detail, but rather to enquire what Professor Auerbach means by the theme of the book as a whole, which is suggested in the title.

Five of the chapters seem to me especially important for understanding Professor Auerbach's theme. The reader inevitably wants to know how "reality" and "representation" are understood. Professor Auerbach does not define either term, for his method is to concentrate upon the analyses of particular texts, and to rely upon the reader to derive his understanding of the general ideas from common sense and from the material itself. Thus his concept "reality" is based upon Dante's Aristotelian-Christian realism, and also modern realism as exemplified in the French novel of the nineteenth century. His notion of representation rests upon the distinction between the classic notion of three separate styles, the elevated, middle, and low, and realistic styles (both medieval and modern) in which the sublime, the everyday, and the low, or grotesque, or comic, or disgusting, are mixed. The five chapters in which these ideas are clearest are 1, Odysseus' Scar; 8, Farinata and Cavalcante; 15, The *Faux Dévot;* 18, In the Hôtel de la Mole, and 19, Germinie Lacerteux.

The first chapter begins with an analysis of the episode in the *Odyssey* in which Odysseus' old nurse, Eurycleia, giving him a bath, recognizes him by a scar on his thigh. What Professor Auerbach has to say about the way reality is represented in this episode: its bright, uniform illumination; its rigidly-held present tense—for the interpolation which recounts Odysseus' wounding by the boar, years ago, is as present as the bath—the sensuous immediacy of everything; the serenity of the narrative movement—is very just and illuminating. But the point of the chapter is clear only when the Homeric episode is compared with the Abraham-Isaac story in the Old Testament. In reading Homer, "It does not matter whether we know that all this is only legend, 'make-believe.' The oft-repeated reproach that Homer is a liar takes nothing from his effectiveness, he does not need to base his story on historical reality." The Old Testament narrative, on the contrary, is rooted in time and history; in Abraham's past, and in the past of his tribe. It is far darker and more mysterious than Homer; all is directed toward the partly-hidden will of God; but it offers itself as literally true. Because of this basic attitude to its reality, the tiniest episode, however humble or grotesque, may be as "problematic" (one of the author's favorite words), as significant and intense, as the sublimest tragedy. Because it is true, mysterious, and related at every point to the will of God, it requires, and has of course received, endless interpretation. Homer, on the other hand, being immediately clear, completely expressed, neither requires nor admits interpretation. The Old Testament story represents reality much more than Homer does; Homer, though he wrote before the classic doctrine of the separation of styles, stands for that

213

classic conception of art which Professor Auerbach uses throughout to contrast with the various kinds of realism.

The full scope of Professor Auerbach's conception of the Hebraic-Christian realism does not emerge until he comes to Dante. Chapter 8, on the Farinata-Cavalcante episode in the *Inferno,* is offered as an example of Dante's realism, or, as it may be described, his *mixture* of styles. The point is that Dante can compass both common speech and the humblest subjects, classically associated with comedy, and at the same time the most "sublime" emotions and rhetorical effects, classically associated with tragedy and epic. Dante's realism, like that of the Old Testament, is religious: it is the eye of God upon every detail of human life which guarantees its timeless value and meaning, yet at the same time firmly anchors it in time and place. Religious realism in this tradition deals with human individual fates of all kinds. The classic notion of three styles, on the other hand, tends to be general, typical, moralistic, or "esthetic." It is usually associated with a rigid class structure, and the low style for servants, the high style for princes, is supposed to reflect some natural and permanent stratification in human society. The *Divine Comedy* and the Old Testament narratives, on the other hand, envisage a "reality" much more fundamental than any social order, any abstract moral system, or any absolute conception of style.

Professor Auerbach's conception of this religious realism, starting in the Old Testament and culminating in Dante, contains, I think, his most original and illuminating insights. It would not be possible to do justice to it in a review; I'm not even sure that *Mimesis* makes it sufficiently clear. The early book on Dante, the monograph, *Figura,* in which the development of Dante's realism from its ancient sources is traced, and a number of shorter studies of Dante's methods which have appeared in various journals, would perhaps be required for full understanding of Professor Auerbach's views. I hope that this material will soon be collected and made available in English, for I think it is of first importance in our present literary studies.

I have more reservations about the application of these concepts to more modern literature in the remainder of the book. Chapter 15, The *Faux Dévot* (one of La Bruyère's *Caractères*) is in effect a brief study of French neoclassicism in relation to Professor Auerbach's theme. In general, he sees the age of Louis XIV as governed by the classic "separation of styles" with all that goes with it—the sense of reality, as one might put it, strained through social, moral, and esthetic conventions. It is this chapter, therefore, where one may best study the classic or neoclassic conception of literary representation which Professor Auerbach opposes to realism. The reservations I have are due less to the author's native understanding of this literature than to the focus of the book as a whole, which is not well designed to bring out what Racine and Molière, for example, do offer. Professor Auerbach, following his line of enquiry, does not seek to expound what *they* achieved, so much as to estimate their "realism." Even from this point of view one might have questions: is there no "reality" in Molière's rational norms, conventional though they are, or in Racine's moral paradoxes, abstract though *they* are?—It depends, of course, upon what one means by reality.

In chapters 18 and 19 Professor Auerbach discusses Stendhal, Balzac, Flaubert, the Goncourts and Zola; and these chapters, taken together, show what is meant by modern realism. Modern realism is quite different from Dante's, yet Professor Auerbach accepts it as "real" also, and perhaps even more real. He defines it as follows: "The serious treatment of everyday reality, the rise of more extensive and socially inferior human groups to the position of subject matter for problematic-existential representation, on the one hand; on the other, the embedding of random persons and events in the general course of contemporary history, the fluid historical background—these, we believe, are the foundations of modern realism" (page 491). I do not quarrel with this definition, nor with the fine analyses of passages from particular works. If these chapters do not quite satisfy me, that is perhaps because we have so much modern realism which fulfills the definition, yet strikes me as insignificant and not very "real." Are the differentia of this school or style as significant as Professor Auerbach seems to maintain? Do we not usually, and rightly, think that the best modern realists are those who reveal most about human nature and destiny *beyond* the temporal facts, and who construct the most rich and satisfying poetic forms?

Such questions as these are perhaps inappropriate, because of the focus and method of the whole of *Mimesis*. But raising them may help us to understand the point of view which gives the book its great scope, its kind of objectivity, and its deep, if hidden, consistency. There is, for example, the view of history and its importance which is implied in Professor Auerbach's definition of modern realism. In Dante's realism history has its crucial place, but so do moral truth and God, the ultimate object of faith and hope; both of them are outside the temporal sequence itself, though in perpetual relation to it. If God is not in the picture at all, and the "truths" of the moral life vary with the shifts of time and place and circumstance, then "history" is the ultimate reality. The modern realists' concern with "the general course of contemporary history, the fluid historical background," would make their realism realer than Dante's—for his view of the shifting scenes of history is formed by his belief in the timeless realities of God and moral truth. For the purposes of *Mimesis* as a whole, Professor Auerbach has accepted, I think, the view that history is the realest or final reality. This does not prevent him from appreciating Dante to the full—on the contrary; but it makes it unnecessary, and even irrelevant, to compare Dante's realism with Flaubert's: the relation is historic. There is, as I suggested, a *kind* of objectivity in this view; Professor Auerbach speaks at one point of the "incomparable historical vantage point which [this age] affords." But questions of permanent value, whether moral, artistic, or religious, are ruled out.

Questions of artistic value are ruled out too. I must hasten to say that this does not mean that Professor Auerbach fails to see artistic values; his poetic sensibility is evident again and again, it is one of the things that give *Mimesis* its great value. But he is investigating the representation of reality and not poetry as such. For that reason he never raises the questions which chiefly concern modern American criticism: the unity and coherence of the poem or play as a whole, the integrity and inner order of the art-work. That is one reason why his method of analyzing short passages from longer works is so effective for his purposes: he wants to know, not what the author made, but how he represents a reality outside the poem altogether. It is amazing how much this method reveals incidentally about poetry and poems. But from time to time it leads Professor Auerbach to judgments which I question, for example, that Dante's characters are so real that the coherence of the Canto or Cantica is lost: I should prefer to say that the larger units of the composition are there to be seen, if one is looking for them. His treatment of Shakespeare, based on the analysis of a short scene between Prince Hal and Poins, though it illustrates his theme well and most interestingly, is hardly adequate for Shakespeare. His unit is the play; I do not think one can assess his success in representing reality on the basis of a shorter selection.

The great value of *Mimesis* for us lies in its unfashionable focus: it is time we raised once more the ancient question of art's truth to reality. On the basis of a common-sense and historistic conception of reality, Professor Auerbach has written a work of extraordinary learning, perceptiveness, and rigor. I think its methods, its ideas, and its particular insights should keep us busy for a long time.